To Be
Old and Sad

To Be
Old and Sad
Understanding Depression
in the Elderly

by

NATHAN BILLIG, M.D.

LEXINGTON BOOKS
An Imprint of Macmillan, Inc.
NEW YORK

Maxwell Macmillan Canada
TORONTO

Maxwell Macmillan International
NEW YORK   OXFORD   SINGAPORE   SYDNEY

Lexington Books
An Imprint of Macmillan, Inc.
866 Third Avenue, New York, N.Y. 10022

Maxwell Macmillan Canada, Inc.
1200 Eglinton Avenue East
Suite 200
Don Mills, Ontario M3C 3N1

Macmillan, Inc. is part of the Maxwell Communication
Group of Companies.

Printed in the United States of America

printing number
6 7 8 9 10

Library of Congress Cataloging-in-Publication Data

Billig, Nathan.
To be old and sad.

Includes index.
1. Depression in the aged.   I. Title.
RC537.5.B55   1987   618.97′68527   85–45736
ISBN 0–669–12277–7 (alk. paper)
ISBN 0–669–12279–3 (pbk. : alk. paper)

In honor of my children
Deborah Karen Billig
Andrew Swire Billig
Peter Jonas Billig
and

In memory of my parents
Anna and Abraham Billig

Contents

Preface and Acknowledgments

To Be Old and Sad is about older people and about depression. Those may seem like depressing subjects, but they don't have to be so. Older people are rich in history, knowledge, wisdom, and skills that are often limited or lost because of the affliction of depression. This is a hopeful book that focuses on the benefits of treating the most common disorder of adult life.

This book grows out of my interest in the elderly and their medical and psychological problems. The elderly have few advocates and the depressed elderly even fewer. In my work as a practicing geriatric psychiatrist I have talked with elderly patients and their families over a number of years, helping them cope with problems, frustrations, misdiagnoses, misconceptions, and often inadequate treatment. We have looked for better ways to treat a treatable illness.

I intend this book as a practical, informative, supportive work geared to families with elderly members and to older adults who are concerned about the possibility of depression in themselves, in friends, and in family members and who want to learn more about its origins, symptoms, and treatment. It is also intended for students in fields concerned with elderly adults and for practitioners in medicine, counseling, nursing, and other helping professions.

I am indebted to many people. My patients have taught me most of what is in this book. They continue to enrich me both professionally and privately.

Dr. Gene D. Cohen, Dr. Barry Lebowitz, Dr. Louis F. Rittelmeyer, Jr., Dr. David L. Rabin, and Dr. John C. Harvey have much to do with my being a geriatric psychiatrist and I am grateful for their support of my research and clinical work at Georgetown.

The idea for this book was nurtured by Dr. Kathleen C. Buckwalter. Ms. Anne Edelstein of Writers House was a continuing source of support, enthusiasm, and practical advice, which made writing this book possible. Stuart Dunn, Dr. Stephen Green and Dr. Cecile Dunn read parts of the manuscript and offered critical comments. My family was patient and understanding over the years of planning and writing. Margaret Zusky of Lexington Books enthusiastically supported this project. Donelle O'Meara typed the manuscript, edited the copy, and gave useful suggestions along the way.

Dr. Gail G. Weinmann deserves a special acknowledgment for her consistently wise advice, patience, constant support, and encouragement over many months.

To all I am grateful.

To Be
Old and Sad

1

To Be Old and Sad:
Some Background

"To be old and sad is double jeopardy," said an 85-year-old retired attorney who was increasingly aware of the disability of his depression.

A 78-year-old woman who until recently was active in her community, shopped, drove her car to visit friends, enjoyed movies and plays, and remembered most of the mathematical principles she taught for 35 years, described herself as "over the hill, having lived enough and too old to keep on going."

THESE two statements epitomize the expressions of sadness, hopelessness, helplessness, and decreasing self-worth that can be depression in the elderly. What is this condition? Is it inevitable that when you get old you get depressed? What does depression have to do with Alzheimer's disease, senility, and other conditions associated with old age? Does depression mean you're crazy? Is depression treatable?

These are questions that often occur to older people who feel blue or sad, or worse. These questions may not be asked openly and therefore are rarely fully answered. Growing older does have its difficulties and they should be acknowledged, but reaching 65 or 75 or even 85 years of age does not have to mean that "life is not worth living."

Approximately 12 percent of the population was over the age of 65 in 1986. By the year 2020, that group will approach 20 percent of the total population. Arbitrarily it is said that 65 is the beginning of "the later years." When we talk or think about the "elderly" we are talking about a large group that covers a wide span—from age 65 to perhaps 100 or more. There is no other age group that extends over so much time and none that is more diverse in physical or mental functioning. The older a person is, the more variable are his or her characteristics. We all have certain biological predispositions that are influenced and molded by years of experience in a number of areas of life. As we age we are continuously changed by relationships, events, and experiences. Seventy-year-olds are much more different from each other than are 5-year-olds or 15-year-olds. In fact we would find it most difficult to describe a typical 70-year-old.

It is hazardous, then, to describe more than the general patterns that exist in a given time of life, especially in the later years. We must acknowledge that there is considerable room for variability. There are 75-year-olds who look like 60-year-olds and 75-year-olds who look like 90-year-olds. We know that 75-year-olds are administering law firms, enjoying well-earned retirements, or doing volunteer work. There are also 75-year-olds who are incapacitated by illness, readying for the grave, or have otherwise given up on living. These characteristics are based on a large number of factors that include genetic, environmental, biological, and social elements.

The older adult can look back on a history that is rich in experiences—some are undoubtedly sad, others joyful. There are always accomplishments and failures, struggles and times of ease. The mentally healthy adult can usually appraise these in some reasonable way, accepting with sadness and regret the losses and sufferings, and valuing the achievements. The trap of depression is not necessarily integral to the aging process. Although extremely common, depression does *not* happen to all older people and should not be any more acceptable as a state of health than is pneumonia.

We hear of old people "being given permission" to be dysfunctional with depression because they have severe arthritis, have had a stroke, or because their children live at a great distance. No one is really entitled to be depressed because of a hard life, chronic illness, or many losses. It would be double jeopardy or worse to have one of these problems and to be depressed! Such problems are surely upsetting issues for many, and a person who has endured great difficulty may be blue or sad, but not necessarily depressed, hopeless, or helpless. If we give permission to ourselves or to our elderly friends or relatives to be depressed, if we accept that growing older includes growing depressed, if we ignore the signs and symptoms of a treatable illness, we are depriving ourselves and those close to us of opportunities to enjoy, to reminisce, and to have a continuing sense of purpose that certainly can be what growing older is about.

All of us have heard, "He's doing pretty well for a 75-year-old." That concept is invalid. It reflects the expectation that a 75-year-old should generally be doing poorly. There's no scientific basis for that notion, and in some respects the opposite is true. Someone who has negotiated through 75 years in this world has some basic strengths, both physically and mentally. Why don't we focus on the expectations that derive from *that* notion? Those of us who are generally optimistic benefit from a point of view based on assets, strengths, collected experiences, reminiscences, and functional abilities that are most commonly a part of growing older.

Depression is surely something with which many older adults must contend. It is not just sadness. It is a clinical problem, a syndrome, a disorder made up of a set of symptoms which mean that something is not right with the affected person. Most elderly are not depressed, but unfortunately up to 15 to 20 percent of older people are. Most of these suffer in silence, and remain undiagnosed, misdiagnosed, and most importantly, untreated. Depression is a rampant disorder at all ages; in fact, it is the most common psychiatric problem. Because depression is more prevalent in the elderly population than in any other age group, it represents a major mental health, medical, and social problem that may potentially touch us all.

The problem of depression in the elderly is compounded by the fact that it is one of the great masqueraders of medicine. Depression in older adults, unlike in younger people, frequently first shows itself as a physical problem—headaches, low back pain, chest symptoms, bowel disturbances—and may not be thought of as a primary problem to be treated. In fact, depression is often not considered by medical and even mental health personnel, and so many patients are dismissed as "just complainers" or people who "don't have enough to do." If depression were recognized as the clinical problem that might be causing or exaggerating some of the physical symptoms, it could be treated, and perhaps the result would be the relief of many of the symptoms that seem so distressing to patient and doctor alike.

Depressed older adults are often brought to medical attention with complaints of memory failure, disorientation, and confusion. They appear, even to their doctors, to have a brain disorder such as Alzheimer's disease; they do not appear depressed. For some of these people, however, depression is the major problem. In these cases, depression is masquerading as an organic brain disease or is possibly aggravating an existing mild dementia. If the depression is not recognized, it cannot be treated, and the patient may be inappropriately written off as demented, given a much less hopeful diagnosis, and possibly relegated to custodial care. Unlike Alzheimer's disease, depression can be treated successfully using a number of therapeutic techniques.

In addition to masquerading as a medical problem, depression can appear as a result or symptom of a primary medical problem. It can be the consequence of medications, a medical illness, or a combination of these. For instance, although a younger person usually experiences shortness of breath and lethargy as the initial symptoms of heart failure, an older adult may present a "sense of dread" or depression as an early symptom of a heart condition. The same complaints may precede some cancers and gastrointestinal, pulmonary, cardiovascular, and other medical problems. It is not known why this happens and it is not a common occurrence, but physicians and patients must recognize the possibility that the symptoms of depression sometimes declare the onset of a medical problem.

Like younger people, older adults are certainly not immune to the pent-up feelings of frustration and loss that they have not adequately dealt with earlier in their lives. In the elderly these feelings are compounded by the real losses of productivity, mobility, companionship, and health that often come with advancing age.

Depression frequently does not arise anew after age 65. Rather, if we look more closely, we often see that the latest problem is reminiscent of an earlier episode or pattern of depressive periods. The family may have a history of depressive problems. It is important to know this and to find out if the problem was treated and how it was treated. There is some indication that depression is more common in some families and is recurrent in some individuals. This may mean that some people have a biological predisposition that could be expressed with varying stresses.

Depression in the older adult is complex and involves the biology of aging, the mixture of losses and successes throughout life, the interplay of medical illnesses and their treatments, and the strengths and weaknesses that make up the person. Depression results from a number of factors and produces diverse symptoms. A comprehensive medical and psychological evaluation is required to make an accurate diagnosis so that a treatment plan can be initiated.

The picture for the large number of depressed elderly is not as grim as it may seem. Depression is one of the most treatable problems that physicians encounter. Unfortunately, the present generation of elderly don't eagerly seek psychiatric evaluation and treatment, and sometimes view psychotherapy or medications for psychological conditions as being reserved for "crazy people," the unfortunates of the world, or rich faddists who talk about their shrinks at parties. "Getting old is depressing and that's all there is to it," one resigned older woman said to me. In fact, an expanding number of therapies have been highly successful with the elderly, and getting old is not depressing for most people. If aging is depressing, something is wrong!

The following chapters explore evaluation, diagnosis, and treatment to demonstrate that depression—far from being a vague feeling or a catastrophic illness that needs to be endured or denied—is a serious clinical problem of some complexity that has causes, signs and symptoms, and is eminently treatable.

2

Why Are They So Vulnerable?

"You know, Doctor, I'm not 81 anymore. I'm getting old," said an 84-year-old woman who was just becoming aware of the vulnerabilities of old age.

M ANY people regard late life and depression as being synonymous. They are not. But behind that myth lies the important issue of the relationship between old age and one's vulnerability to depression. It is known that with normal aging, from about age 30, there are small but progressive losses of lung, kidney, liver, and other bodily functions. With these losses of function come a loss of flexibility in dealing with unusual demands on the body; thus it may be more difficult to recover from a viral infection or heal from surgery. Similarly, the aging person may lose flexibility in dealing with mental stress and may be more vulnerable to psychological problems. Our vulnerability has to do with a combination of physical and environmental predispositions on the one hand and the stresses that we encounter on the other.

Flexibility and Coping

We all recognize that, as we age, we, our parents, and grandparents tend to be less flexible in our schedules, activities, diets, and general patterns of living. This may make us more susceptible to the inevitable surprises, crises, or changes that come about over the years. At the same time we may also demonstrate a decrease in our usually adaptive coping skills, which helped us better deal with stresses in the past. Hard work, athletics, and other physical outlets, for example, may have to be adjusted to a level that is more suitable to a person's physical status. Impairments in hearing, vision, and taste, and decreases in stamina may add to the generalized feeling that coping ability is decreasing. "The body doesn't seem to work as well as it used to," an 80-year-old woman said to me. Indeed, she had to eat more carefully so that she didn't get indigestion, her arthritis "reminded her" every morning of where all the joints were in her body, and she thought she just didn't look as good as she did at 50! All of these changes and others don't necessarily mean that one is *ill;* rather they mean that some parts are wearing and that one has to cope with those changes and the potential vulnerability they bring.

Biological Changes

Established data suggests that there are changes in the amounts of some brain chemicals (neurotransmitters) as aging proceeds. The relative decreases in some of these chemicals and the increases in others may have some role in predisposing the elderly to depression. Likewise, hormones—including those from the adrenal, thyroid, and pituitary glands—may change in quantity and quality during aging and may account for a greater susceptibility to depression. This area is being investigated widely and new information about the biology of depression will be available over the next few years.

Developmental Issues

Erik Erikson, a noted psychoanalyst and researcher, views old age as a stage of life that involves a struggle of "ego integrity versus despair." By ego integrity he means "the acceptance of one's own and only life cycle; . . . an acceptance of the fact that one's life is one's own responsibility." In other words, successfully reaching old age includes coming to terms with one's positive and negative experiences and not hoping that things, relationships, and experiences can be remade to make up for the past. If one cannot achieve this level of integrity, despair wins out. Integrity is clearly easier if one has successfully mastered earlier developmental stages and can draw on a wide range of gratifying experiences and a history of flexibility to meet the inevitable changes in physical status, age, health, and the other uncertainties that we all encounter with time.

Losses

Inherent in the aging process is the concept and reality of loss. We lose not only some bodily functions and stamina, but we also may lose friends and loved ones, status, financial stability, health, and some of the acuity of our senses. Losses are inevitable; they are a part of everyone's life experience. They present a larger challenge to our coping skills than any set of emotional experiences. In an elderly person, the losses are cumulative and intense. Most people can deal with loss successfully although it may be difficult. Depression may become a clinical problem when a person is overwhelmed with losses without the ability to cope with them.

It may not only be current losses that predispose people to depression, but also the reliving of losses sustained earlier in life that were not satisfactorily worked through, mourned, or otherwise dealt with. They may resurface because of some current reminder and then complicate our present mental state, making us more vulnerable to depression in the here and now. I am reminded of the poignant experience of a vigorous 83-year-old man who came to see me for depression. He said incidentally that he had recently given up one of his favorite pleasures, golf, because his three regular golfing partners had died within the past year. He had not only lost three friends, but had in addition given up one of his most enjoyable avocations. He needed to mourn those losses and others, which he did in brief psychotherapy. Later he found a creative partial solution through meeting a teen-age neighbor whose game the older man could help improve.

Social Issues

The social system in which older adults find themselves is of vital importance in assessing their vulnerability to psychological problems, and to depression in particular. Because of the losses of loved ones and friends, the support system that had become increasingly important over the years may now be considerably diminished and the elderly person may be relatively isolated. Widows and widowers may retreat into a virtually solitary existence. As physical stamina decreases and chronic illness intrudes itself as a major stressor, activities that had been part of the usual week's schedule become more difficult to enjoy, especially if they have to be done without company or require more planning for assistance. Children and grandchildren develop their own lives, friends, and families, and older people may say, "We don't want to be a burden. We want them to live their own lives." Indeed, our society is very much youth oriented, and until very recent years we scarcely focused on problems of the aged, the complexities of their health and social needs, the catastrophe of Alzheimer's disease, and the dilemmas of nursing home placement. The extended family no longer lives under one roof, and most families no longer offer the intimate contact of two, three, or even four generations and the inherent support and security of that environment.

Retirement

Retirement, for many, offers an opportunity for some "golden years" after many years of work. It allows time for the extended vacations that might not have been taken earlier, relative freedom from responsibilities for children, the chance to try some new vocation or avocation, and an opportunity to spend time with one's spouse, friends of many years, and adult children and grandchildren. Retirement works this way for many people, particularly if they are relatively healthy, have some financial resources, have good relationships or the potential to develop them, and have planned to some extent how they would spend those ten or twenty or more golden years.

Unfortunately, for some people, retirement is not so golden. In fact, it is another reminder of loss. Retirement may provoke marital tension, which may be new or may be uncovered as a result of the extended time together, and it often necessitates a move away from a long-familiar geographic environment. Retirement stresses can make one more vulnerable to depression. This stage of life can be planned to a great extent, and to be successful it should be approached in a structured way, particularly for people who have difficulty with the kinds of changes, choices, and flexibility that retirement from active work may bring.

Medical Problems

Medical illness is not pleasant to endure at any age, and for the older adult it is even more difficult. Although most older people are not sick, the prevalence of chronic illness is great. They cope less well than their children and grandchildren and find it harder to recuperate. For many, even a rather minor illness is regarded as a signal that their life has taken a major turn for the worse. We often hear an elderly person predicting, "I'll never leave the hospital alive," when there is no medical justification for that kind of gloom. One man with emphysema, which was certainly debilitating but not life-threatening, asked that I "just let him die." He wasn't close to death, and there was nothing we could do or stop doing to let him die. He was seriously depressed, and that condition was compounded by his emphysema and the sense of fragility with which many older people must cope. Hip fractures, cataracts, and the surgery required to treat them are stresses that many elderly people endure, but that may serve as focal points for the onset of depression. Physicians and other professionals involved in those traumas can be alert to the possibility of depression and actively treat it if it occurs. Similarly, there is now significant evidence that more than 50 percent of people who sustain strokes may become depressed in the two years following that catastrophic event. The onset of depression in these situations may be caused by a combination of the organic damage of the stroke and the psychological trauma that ensues.

We often hear, "She was fine until she had that gall bladder surgery," or "He wasn't ever depressed until he had the flu last winter and he hasn't been the same since." Illness and surgery can be triggers that seem to make people more vulnerable. They probably do not cause depression, but rather make one more susceptible when reserves are low, when coping skills are decreased, and when stress is great. Other triggers or risk factors include the recent death of loved ones and friends, alcohol abuse, a change of living situation, an "anniversary reaction" to a previous loss, a move, financial problems, or the loss of a pet.

Medications

Medication is taking on more and more importance in the advancement of medical science, and is of course valuable in the treatment of illness. Medication plays a very important part in the lives of older adults. I have known people to take as many as 16 different medicines dispensed in 42 pills per day. That is quite a task! I often wonder how much medicine can realistically be taken correctly by any one person.

Although medication is in many cases essential to survival, and at other times is helpful in relieving symptoms, we are coming to understand that at times medications—alone or in combination—produce dangerous or at least unpleasant side effects. Depression is one of those possible adverse effects. The medications most commonly implicated inlcude the antihypertensives, cardiac antiarrhythmics, anti-inflammatory agents, steroids, and beta-blocking agents. This doesn't mean that if you or someone you know is taking one or more of these medications that you will become depressed, nor should you stop taking the drugs if you do develop side effects. Rather, physicians and patients need to be alert to the possibility that any medication *might* be causing mental changes, such as depression, and thoroughly investigate to find the cause. Many medications are available to treat any one medical condition, and medications can sometimes be switched after consultation with the family physician. In other situations a physician may be able to lower the dose of a medication to deal with troublesome side effects.

Mental changes may occur soon after a new medication is added or they may happen after a drug has been used for many years without difficulty. As people age, there are changes in the ways that medicine and other substances are absorbed, metabolized, and eliminated. Geriatricians note that, at times, medications that were once required for a patient's particular problem seem to be no longer needed. Perhaps the system in some way corrects itself—or perhaps the medicine was not needed initially! Just because Uncle Joe got depressed while taking a particular medication does not mean that Aunt Helen will. That medication may suit her best. Individual biological characteristics clearly play a role in this matter. All of these issues must be taken into account in any medical regimen, and medications must be regularly reviewed for their possible side effects and for their continued efficacy and necessity. *When dealing with the older adult, a doctor often does more good by taking away a medication than by adding a new one.*

Reserve Capacity

At any age a person is more vulnerable when his reserve capacity for dealing with stress is diminished. A young, healthy, athletic, nonsmoking man, for example, can be expected to recover relatively easily from viral pneumonia or an appendectomy. This mentally and physically healthy young man might also be expected to weather his failure on an exam or the dissolution of a relationship with another person. He has great physical and emotional reserves, so that reasonable stresses are manageable with appropriate healing, mourning, and recovery. Older people also may have substantial reserves, particularly if they have enjoyed good health, are not poor, are not lonely, have not sustained too many losses, have relationships with people and see or speak to them regularly, and can basically take care of their daily needs or require only minimal assistance. A tall order? Not really. Most older adults function well most of the time. Obviously, the more assets and the fewer deficits one has, the greater the reserve. The stresses impinging on an elderly person can be substantial. Symptoms such as depression may arise when the stresses, either temporarily or over a long period, overwhelm the coping reserves that are available.

Family members or friends often recognize these situations and may play important roles in buoying up their elders whose reserves are being unduly taxed. Family may be able to lend some coping skills to help older people get through a difficult situation, so that despair and depression can be warded off. Such a situation occurred with a woman who moved several hundred miles to be closer to her family, only to find that her family members were less attentive than she had anticipated. By moving, she had given up close companions of twenty or more years, a familiar environment, and supportive work and recreational activities. In her new apartment, in a modern building, she was surrounded by young professional couples and few people of her own age and background. She became increasingly withdrawn, despairing, lonesome for her old setting, and unmotivated to help herself as she had been able to do in the past. A granddaughter, noting the change, acted quickly to engage the woman and help her become more familiar with the new neighborhood and with what it had to offer. This rather minor supportive intervention helped the grandmother overcome her crisis and allowed her to begin to function again. In some ways the intervention was more symbolic than real, but the grandmother felt less hopeless. In time she sought short-term counseling to learn to approach her son and daughter-in-law with more realistic expectations. A potential major depression may have been averted in this relatively well-functioning woman.

Thoughts of Death

Although not necessarily consciously, many older people have some preoccupation with the knowledge that they are closer to death than they have ever been. They feel, perhaps for the first time, perhaps in a more poignant way than previously, that death is a probability in the not-too-distant future. This understanding is rarely voluntarily or openly addressed by older people, but it is obvious to even the most healthy that they are more vulnerable, less strong, and their contemporary friends and relatives are dying. It is debatable how, when, or if this should be broached. There is an axiom in psychiatry that some denial of the facts may be protective and useful to the individual, particularly to the physically ill. But there are times when a person, young or old, is preoccupied with an upsetting thought—death is a common one—and would welcome the simple acknowledgment of that thought. Some people might be ready for broader discussions of their thoughts, feelings, or fears about death; having someone available to listen could be a great relief. Unfortunately, too few of us can tolerate that kind of involvement. I mention this now, not to encourage or discourage family members from discussing these issues, but rather to emphasize that unexpressed thoughts of death can be very real for older adults and represent another source of vulnerability to depression. Talk of death does not have to be a taboo subject.

A 73-year-old man, Mr. A, who "looked younger than his age" was brought to a geriatric psychiatry clinic because he seemed more "clingy and demanding of his wife's time." His adult son thought that his father was depressed. Mr. A seemed to resent his wife spending "his time" with her friends or in activities that seemed trivial to him. The older gentleman had owned and operated a chain of several stores until his retirement five years earlier. He had been in good health until two years before this visit, when in the course of one year he had had a total hip replacement for arthritis and then required cataract surgery. These two surgical traumas made Mr. A painfully aware, for the first time, of his frailty. He became "more of a loner" and said that it was "too late" to make new friends. He reminisced about old high school friends, many of whom had died in the past few years. When he was asked about his worries about dying, he said, "Whenever the good Lord decides to take me, I guess that will be time," denying he had any concerns. It seemed to the staff that Mr. A, because of several recent traumas and losses, had become more dependent, was worried that his infirmities since age 70 represented "the beginning of the end," and was depressed. Psychotherapy was recommended, and Mr. A accepted the idea with some relief because he could talk about his "aches and pains" without upsetting his wife. With time he was able to be less preoccupied with his death, which might not occur for twenty years or more.

Recurrent Depression

Although I have detailed particular vulnerabilities that may occur in the later years, a large group of people have been depressed all their lives, or at least since much earlier in their lives, and have recurrences in late life. A variety of possible causes may be responsible for their symptoms, ranging from early psychological traumas to biological predispositions. Biological causes may be indicated by other family members who are depressed and/or troubled with repetitive or chronic episodes at various times in their lives. The stresses of late life are surely relevant here, may precipitate any given depressive episode, and need to be considered with those elderly for whom depression is recurrent.

Obviously, a complex network of factors can conspire to produce or precipitate depression in the older person. Fortunately they rarely all converge. Nowhere is the interweaving of biological (including genetic), sociocultural, medical, and psychological issues so apparent. Susceptibility and vulnerability are important to acknowledge, to watch for, and to assist with when possible. They do not imply a chronic mental illness or doom. Rather, they represent a predisposition to a treatable illness that may express itself in signs and symptoms. To these we must be attentive.

3

Signs and Symptoms
of Depression

"I'm not depressed. I just don't feel like living; I'm of no use to anyone."

"I don't know what you mean by 'depressed.' My problem is that my bowels aren't working right and my head aches all the time."

ALTHOUGH the words may not always be the same, the sentiments expressed are common. Older adults who are depressed often deny it, or at least they don't use the word. Depression may not be a word that the current generation of elderly feel as comfortable with as do their children and grandchildren. It is possible that depression is sometimes not really understood as an affect or feeling to be described, so that the abnormal state is accepted, even by the older person who is feeling it, as "just old age." Nonetheless, family members, friends, and helping professionals should be alert to the idea of depression if an older person has chronic physical complaints that don't seem to have a physical basis and expresses or feels profound sadness, such as not wanting to live or feeling of no use to anyone. Sometimes the onset of depression is marked by subtle signs of worry or changes in personality or behavior, which are notable because they are not consistent with that individual's usual way of reacting or thinking. "He's more jittery, worries all the time about little things and he's never been like that; he talks about being poor and yet we have plenty of money," one patient's spouse told me. What else can we look for in our elderly friends and family members that tell us that they are depressed?

Clinicians refer to "signs and symptoms" when they speak of the clues that help them diagnose depression. "Signs" mean the objective indications of a problem—in this case depression—that can be observed by other people in the environment. "Symptoms" are the subjective changes or complaints that are felt or reported by the patient. The signs and symptoms are what the clinician—whether a family physician, psychiatrist, or other professional—will be assessing in an effort to define and diagnose the problem. Depression has some signs and symptoms that are universal and cut across age groups; other indications are peculiar to the elderly. Clinicians must persevere in their investigations to discover the signs and symptoms that might point to depression, in the face of frequent denial and obfuscation, as epitomized by the two quotations at the beginning of this chapter.

Signs

What does the depressed elderly person look like? An array of signs may be present in various combinations over a period of time. When you spend a lot of time with someone you often miss some of the gradual changes in appearance that might be occurring. A relative or friend visiting after weeks or months might say, "grandma looks terrible," and this may be the first clue that grandma is ill, or for that matter, depressed. Depressed people may not take care of their hair, teeth, and skin as well as they had previously, and may generally look unkempt. They may say, when questioned about it, that they don't care what they look like, or "I just don't have the energy to do it," or they may be oblivious to their inattention to

toileting and self care. The husband of one 69-year-old undiagnosed depressed woman complained that his wife "had a
closet full of clothes," but she insisted on wearing the same
purple dress every day unless it was removed from her room.
In prior years she had been "fastidious in every way" and took
great pride in her appearance and dress. The change was one
of the first indications that she was depressed.

Depressed people look sad, although they may not complain
about being sad. They may be frequently teary, or may cry
for no apparent reason or over sad events that occurred many
years ago. They may openly speak of suicide or say "that it
would be just as well if I were hit by a car." They may with-
draw from activities or seem to be just going through the mo-
tions of participating, even in major family occasions such as
a wedding or the arrival of a new grandchild. Their past joys
are no longer enjoyable and their stories of the "good old days"
don't sound so good anymore. When you try to remember
what an older person was like six months or a year ago, you
are forced to think how much he or she has aged in such a
short time. That is an important observation, an important
clue, because people—unless they are quite ill physically—
don't really age that much in half or even a full year. It is as
if they have aged. The appearance of rapid aging is often what
accompanies the diagnosis of depression in an older person.

Depressed people seem slowed down. They appear barely
able to walk from one place to another, as if their feet are
especially heavy. Their entire way of functioning seems to be
in slow motion. Their speech may be distorted in its slowness,
like a record at the wrong speed, or they may not speak very
much at all. They may appear to be tired all the time, but they
also complain that they are unable to sleep. At the other extreme, depressed older adults may be agitated, almost hyper-
active, unable to settle down or relax. They may pace from
one room to another or constantly fidget with a small object.
They may start projects but not complete them. Family members will notice that the depressed person has a change in eating

habits, usually losing his or her appetite and refusing to eat—although overeating is known to occur. Similarily, there usually is a noticeable decrease in sleeping time, with greatly disturbed nights.

Symptoms

Even if the elderly person doesn't complain about depression, he or she will frequently complain about things that can add up to depression. Those complaints generally fall into several common categories that include:

> physical complaints,
>
> emotional symptoms, and
>
> thinking problems.

Physical Complaints

Physical symptoms are in many ways the most prominent complaints of the depressed older person. Older people are known for their "aches and pains" and, indeed, as we age we all have more physical distress. But depressed people become preoccupied with their abdominal distress, headaches, chest pains, arthritic joints, and chronic fatigue. These complaints may mask or disguise depression. What others would accept as a minor distress gets magnified and results in multiple trips to the family physician, numerous tests and X-rays, and few answers. Family physicians become frustrated when they can't seem to diagnose the problem, and may write off the patients as chronic complainers when they don't get better. Some physicians and other professionals will see through the disguise and will entertain the diagnosis of depression when physical complaints increase and no medical diagnosis is apparent.

Other distressing and significant physical complaints include what psychiatrists refer to as "vegetative symptoms," often described as the hallmarks of moderate to severe depression. These are loss of appetite and weight; sleep disturbance, which is often characterized by early morning awakening or multiple awakenings during the night with difficulty in falling back to sleep; constipation; and chronic fatigue.

Sleep disturbances are among the most common complaints of elderly people in general and of depressed people in particular. Although awakening early in the morning, multiple awakenings during the night, and difficulty in falling asleep are the most common complaints, it is also essential to compare these signs to the person's usual sleeping pattern. It is crucial to consider whether sleeping time may be occurring at other times of the day, so that the total hours of sleep are not abnormal, only the timing. One depressed gentleman reported his fear of going to sleep while his wife was asleep. He wanted her to be there in case anything happened to him while he slept. He changed his habits and stayed awake reading and listening to radio talk shows until 4:00 A.M. and then slept until 10:00 or 11:00 A.M. In more usual situations, a considerable amount of day-time napping inhibits night-time sleeping. Sleep disturbances are so discomforting to elderly persons that they often seek, and may abuse, a variety of remedies—some of which may be extremely dangerous. It is vital that changes in sleep patterns or disturbances be carefully attended to by a physician. Some patterns indicate an underlying problem, such as depression; others require some treatment or adjustment to make a better fit with a spouse or social system.

Sexual activity is important to normal older adults, as it is to younger people. Depression often disrupts the usual sexual pattern of the person or couple involved. Rarely, sexual activity is increased, and the spouse or mate senses that the other is especially clingy and dependent and wants to be touching all the time. More usually, however, the depressed person has diminished sexual interest and may complain of impotence. Failure in sexual activity can be a most distressing symptom for the elderly person who has previously enjoyed sex, and is unfortunately a complaint that rarely gets talked about. In this silence, the older adult will not necessarily connect the sexual disturbance with the depression but, rather, will interpret it as another defect to be endured or as further evidence of the deterioration with which he or she must cope.

Alcohol or drug abuse may be a symptom of depression. Although people abuse alcohol and other substances for a number of reasons, one of them is a desperate attempt, consciously or unconsciously, to "medicate" themselves. Unfortunately, alcohol, which is more commonly abused by the elderly than illicit drugs, is a powerful depressant. Older adults may attempt to anesthetize themselves from their depressing or depressed lives, but in fact they are increasing the intensity of the depressive symptoms and complicating their physical and psychological systems with the alcohol abuse. Alcohol has profound effects on the brain, liver, kidneys, and cardiovascular systems, and its abuse often results in an inadequate diet, malnutrition, and poor general hygiene. These then lead to further physical deterioration. People who abuse alcohol may deny it, claiming that they are just having the shot or two their doctors recommended for their hearts' well-being, but friends and family members should seek professional assistance for the older drinker who has a high risk of severe depression and its complications.

Emotional Symptoms

Older people who are depressed don't feel well and sometimes are sad or blue. But they may not describe that feeling as "depression" or even as sadness. They may just say, nonspecifically, that they feel "not right." At other times, one hears rather characteristic expressions of hopelessness, helplessness, and worthlessness, which are among the core emotional symptoms of depression at any age. These statements usually are new for the patient: not what he or she usually sounds like. They are also distortions of the truth. A depressed semiretired lawyer, who had recently successfully handled a rather complex case, began to feel and say that he no longer knew anything about the law, that he was a "fraud," and that he would no longer be able to support his wife and himself in their remaining years. A competent editor refused to take on freelance assignments because she felt that her clients were being cheated by her. She felt that she "really couldn't do anything right." A previously loving grandmother no longer wanted to spend time with her grandchildren.

Worries about money, family, health, responsibilities—worries about everything—become exaggerated in depression. They may often have some basis in reality, but with depression some older people become obsessed with worry and ruminate constantly. They become unable to effectively handle even the usual routine concerns of their lives. Again, what is important to observe is the change from a state that was not characterized by excessive worry to one that is paralyzing or at least very preoccupying. I am reminded of a 73-year-old depressed man who had recently had cataract surgery, recovered well, and resumed his usual activity; but shortly thereafter he became atypically helpless to understand and cope with his medical bills. He worried excessively that they would make him poor and that he would have to give up his house. There was no real basis for these fears. His underlying depression was initiated by the stress of surgery and recovery, and the symptoms of excessive worry were manifestations of that.

Tearing, crying, or having the impulse to cry are symptoms that the older adult may find embarrassing, or inexplicable, or they may be linked to some truly sad event in the recent or distant past. One depressed woman who said that she was tearful "most of her waking hours" told me that it was because she was thinking a great deal about her long-deceased mother. This was not an anniversary, nor was her tearfulness realistically linked to her mother. She was, however, the same age as her mother had been at the time of her death, and in her depression thoughts about death *were* preoccupying. She needed to talk more about those thoughts.

"Emptiness" is frequently expressed by depressed elderly people, as are statements of demoralization. These feelings often coincide with a conviction of uselessness and with suicidal ideas. "I should be thrown in the trash," one man said. The emptiness can take the extreme form of a delusion that "my organs are not right; something is missing in my stomach; there are maggots eating my insides." Sometimes the emptiness is expressed in more symbolic terms, such as by the woman who told me that she felt she was "nothing," she "had no self," she was a "shell."

Although we often think of depressed people as being withdrawn and passive, they may also be irritable, disagreeable, and negativistic—finding fault with things and people that would otherwise have been acceptable. They may not identify this as a problem, but, rather, may attempt to justify their feelings. At other times they may be exceedingly disturbed by their irritability and use it as further evidence of their hopelessness and worthlessness. A previously "easy going" 68-year-old woman became furious with her grandson because he "left a mess" in her car after eating an ice cream cone. She told her daughter that maybe "the kids were too much for her to handle" at this point in her life. The irritability and overreaction to a specific episode were symptoms of her depression. She later felt guilty and increasingly sad that she couldn't cope better with minor stresses.

Thinking (Cognitive) Symptoms

Clinicians as well as laymen too often do not associate thinking distortions or difficulties with depression. Young and old patients may have thought disturbances that are primarily due to clinical depression. A depressed college student may find that he has difficulty concentrating while studying or thinking about the questions on an exam. An older person may not remember her address and telephone number, or may think that the CIA has bugged her house. Thinking disturbances manifested by memory failure, difficulty concentrating, delusions, and hallucinations may be associated with depression as well as with other psychiatric and neurological conditions. When we hear or see these symptoms it is important to distinguish depression from a condition such as Alzheimer's disease, which can present with some similar symptoms. (See also chapter 6.)

The term "pseudo-dementia" has been used to label the dementia-like symptoms of memory loss, language inhibition, difficulty with concentration, diminished learning capacity, and decrease in functioning in the activities of daily living that may accompany depression in the aged. In fact, there is nothing "pseudo" about this condition and I prefer the term "the dementia of depression." At first, it is often difficult to determine whether the dementia is due to an organic brain disorder—something physically wrong with the brain—or to depression. Some clinicians advocate a therapeutic trial period on antidepressant medications, to see if the dementia clears up, thus verifying its origins in depression. Others point out that a large percentage of patients who are primarily demented (i.e., with Alzheimer's disease) are also depressed and that their functioning would improve if treated for depression, even though an underlying dementia would remain. Patients with a dementia of depression tend to have a more rapid onset of the memory impairment; show more fluctuations in functioning during any day, week, or month; give up more easily when questioned during an assessment; and are more consistently depressed than are patients with an organic dementia. These distinctions are subtle, often require extensive observations and evaluation, and it is crucial that those be done to make the most accurate diagnosis.

Sometimes the distortions in thinking are quite dramatic. An elderly woman was "driving her husband crazy" with constant complaints that "there was another couple living in their apartment with them." The exasperated husband could not convince his wife of her distortion and listened to his wife's incessant monologues concerning the intruders and their bad habits. This fixed delusion, or false belief, was one of many symptoms of depression, but was the most alarming in that it appeared to be so inexplicable, so crazy, to family and friends. Very disturbing thoughts such as these are often missed as possible symptoms of depression, and remit when the depression is treated.

Another patient, a man of 78 years, regaled me with his distress that each night someone would come into his house and steal some money. Sometimes "they" would also rearrange his clothing so that he couldn't find his favorite shirt or his slippers the next morning. This gentleman's family thought that he had lost his ability to test reality and was hopelessly "senile." Although he did have some indications of mild dementia, his paranoid delusions were caused by a rather severe depression. The stealing, or losing, could be viewed dynamically as an expression of his generalized sense of loss. Actually, he would sometimes misplace his prized objects or forget where he had put them for safe-keeping, but would attribute his losses to others. Not all delusions in older people are the result of depression, but that possibility should be considered.

Similarly, older adults who are depressed may have hallucinations—sensory perceptions that are not based on reality and are not the result of external stimulation to the senses (i.e., hearing voices that aren't really there). They may smell something in the apartment, although no one else can verify the odor. They may hear voices that tell them private or distressing messages. These sound very crazy to the normal observer, but they are symptoms of some grave distress that we should seriously consider and not pass off as just getting senile.

Older people are sometimes brought to clinicians for the primary symptom of repeating a particular thought, story, or feeling. This can be very distressing to a family member who must endure hearing the same story told over and over again as though it had never been told. It is as if the person forgets that he or she just told you that story, and when reminded, says, "I did? Oh, I'm sorry," and then promptly tells it again! Such people sometimes appear to be inattentive to what they are saying or to how they are perceived. The repeating, dwelling, ruminating may be symptoms of depression or anxiety that may be present.

As at other ages, depressed older adults tend to be self-blaming, overly critical, and pessimistic. They seem to have forgotten the time when they functioned well, or say that they are old, so "what's the use of trying." This line of thinking is dangerous, particularly if the older person feels that there is little to live for. They may actively seek a solution in suicide or may consciously or unconsciously ignore health, nutrition, or safety so that death is made more possible.

Suicidal Thoughts and Deeds: Special Symptoms

Suicide is more common in elderly white men than in any other age group. In women the peak suicide risk is in the immediate postmenopausal period. The elderly population (12 percent) accounts for more than 25 percent of the suicides committed. When older adults attempt suicide they more usually succeed than do people of other ages. Suicide attempts in the elderly should not be dismissed as gestures. They must be taken seriously; they always mean great distress. And most suicides are attempted by people who are depressed or who are just mobilizing from a serious depression. In view of these data, suicide must be reckoned with by the family and the clinician and seriously considered in any evaluation of a depressed older adult.

Suicidal feelings occur, at least fleetingly, in most depressed people and maybe in most people, but the idea of suicide as a solution to one's problems or as a real relief from one's state of mind is a different matter. Even the actively suicidal state is usually temporary, lasting days or weeks, and it needs to be approached as a potentially treatable symptom that is part of a larger problem, usually depression.

Many of the vulnerabilities to suicide are the same as those discussed for depression, but there are also some special risk factors. It should be noted that older adults who attempt suicide often do so impulsively and don't give a clear message of increased distress or of particular desperation. Therefore special vulnerabilities have to be kept in mind. The loss of a spouse is a major risk factor for suicide, and the risk may last for weeks or months, depending on the mourning process and the person's adaptation to widowhood. Older people may feel totally lost in the world without their spouse, unable to contemplate survival, or they may have some variant of the delusion of being called to the dead spouse's grave, "being called to join him." These distinctions have to be made by clinicians because they give us some notion of how irrational and how extensive the feelings of loss may be.

The presence of dementia or other organic mental impairments increases the suicide risk, as does the abuse of alcohol and other drugs. Increased somatic complaints may herald potential suicide; it is well known that most patients who attempt suicide have seen their physicians in the prior month. Most have had physical complaints and have not mentioned suicide or even depression.

What is the role of family, friends or nonpsychiatric clinicians in the face of some suicide risk or threat? Although the question is not always responded to honestly, it is worth asking a worrisome person whether he or she has thought about self-harm or suicide, and if so, how strong is that thought or feeling? Does he or she have a plan to do it? Can he or she talk about the distress? Most people in distress welcome and respond to care, concern, and support. If you feel that someone in danger is unresponsive or resistant to that concern, it is entirely appropriate to enlist the help of others to protect against a potentially avoidable catastrophe. Family physicians, mental health professionals, or, as a last resort, the police should be called to assist in an emergency in which hospitalization is necessary to protect someone from suicide. There are advocates for what has been termed "rational suicide" in cases of terminal illness. For most depressed people the suicide idea or attempt is not rational and should be viewed as a symptom to be treated.

What about the terminally ill patient who expresses the desire to die? It is perhaps surprising that most older people with terminal illnesses do not wish to die, and certainly do not wish to have their lives terminated prematurely by suicide or mercy-killing. Although this area has not been studied extensively, some research indicates that most of those people who wish for an early death are clinically depressed: they exhibit the signs and symptoms that are the criteria for the diagnosis of major depression. Suicidal thought is just one of those symptoms. When confronted by such a patient, clinicians treat the depression before considering issues related to rational suicide.

The signs and symptoms of depression are extensive and cover a wide range of behaviors, feelings, thoughts, and physical functions. Some are more disabling to the patient, and others are more alarming to those observing. A depressed individual may have a few symptoms or a vast array. The diagnosis of depression in the elderly person is made by compiling the person's history, physical examination, evaluation of mental status, and a variety of other possible tests. The signs and symptoms gathered from the history and other evaluations are the clues that lead the clinician to a possible diagnosis and eventually to a proper treatment.

4

What To Do First?
The Process of Evaluation

Mrs. G notices that she hasn't been sleeping as well as usual. She feels tired all the time, even a little sick, with more aches and pains than usual. She's sad, seems tearful, but says, "there's really nothing to be that upset about." Mrs. G is also having trouble thinking clearly and concentrating when she tries to read the newspaper. She tries to think about when it began. She remembers enjoying a vacation a year ago. It was shortly after that vacation that her husband went into the hospital to have a polyp removed from his intestine. "Everything was alright—it was benign, but it was a scare. Maybe things haven't been right since shortly after he recovered." Now he had to be concerned about her; their roles seemed to be changing, and that was hard on both Mrs. G and her husband, she says.

MRS. G describes a feeling or state of depression. But what can be done about it? To whom can she turn? Does she go to the family doctor, or to a psychiatrist or other mental health person? "Or maybe it will just go away and I'll be back to normal again."

Most significantly depressed people who have relationships with others are noticed by family members or friends as being depressed. They try to talk the person out of it: "Look at all the good things in your life; just get busier and everything will be OK." Sometimes they are right. Depression is often time-limited. After weeks or months a particular episode subsides and the person feels better. Everyone has blue days, or longer times when something has happened that causes grief or sadness. But when depression becomes more intense and disabling, those weeks and months can be tough. Sometimes it lasts longer and feels as though it will never end.

Depression in its milder forms may respond well to support from family and friends, and from ventilation through talk, exercise, good diet, socialization, usual activities, or some combination of these. A good response depends somewhat on the causes of the depression, the vulnerabilities of the individual, the available resources, and the individual's coping mechanisms. "Home remedies," when available, are helpful in any situation and certainly should be vigorously used whenever possible. But what about the situations that don't respond to these attempts, where the symptoms seem to deepen or increase in number?

Most depressed older adults go first to their family physician or internist. Many are drawn there by familiarity, others by physical complaints. In either case nonpsychiatric physicians have the opportunity to treat more cases of depression than any other professionals. Some older adults have had prior contact with a psychiatrist or other mental health professional and may wish to consult with one of them. Before treatment, however, an assessment must determine, as well as possible, the causes of this complex problem. It matters less where one starts; it matters a great deal what gets accomplished.

A family member or a friend is often vital to the success of a medical or psychiatric evaluation for depression in an older adult. The interested person may be the prime mover in making the initial appointment and in physically accompanying the prospective elderly patient. It is scary to seek help for "a mental problem," particularly if it is affecting one's ability to think, remember, and concentrate, or if one feels hopeless and worthless. It is somewhat easier if the primary symptoms are physical and the patient can seek medical consultation and deny the "psychiatric" aspects. In either situation, the presence and support of a caring person eases the way. When psychological symptoms are present it can be reassuring to have someone on whom to depend; when physical symptoms predominate the interested person can be a buffer between the often frustrated medical personnel and the patient, who may feel unheard or misunderstood.

From the perspective of the clinician, the family member or friend is a critical source of information. Initially, the patient is almost always anxious in the clinical setting and may not reveal important information about the history of his or her illness. The patient may unconsciously deny issues of great significance that can be presented only by a close relative or friend. That person may also provide information about what is happening in the family or other social environments. In some situations the patient is confused, disoriented, or has some degree of memory impairment and thus, again, the facts of the situation may be incomplete. Older adults frequently have hearing impairments and the presence of a familiar person may ease communication with a relatively unknown clinician. The physician's office, clinic, or hospital may represent a backlog of negative or fearful experiences and therefore the patient may require the active support—indeed, the "push"—of another person to overcome the inertia that prevents people from seeking help.

The symptomatic older person and their family member or friend approach the clinician to get some answers. What they will get first is many questions! The physician or mental health profesional will want to take a history. This means that they will want to learn from the patient everything they can about the person and his or her symptoms. They will systematically inquire about:

the chief complaint—the major problem with which the patient is dealing;

the history of the present illness—a detailed account of everything related to the recent symptoms;

the person's past medical and psychological history;

the family history of medical and psychological problems;

the person's social history—activities, interests, functional abilities, and habits;

and the person's history of illnesses, medications, and hospitalizations.

The clinician will also ask about activities of daily living—the extent to which the person continues to take care of him- or herself. For example, can the patient maintain an apartment, shop, cook, pay bills, use a telephone, socialize, and take care of basic needs like feeding, dressing, and toileting? How have these activities changed? These activities and accomplishments are an important guide to one's ability to function, and are essential to assess when judging the extent to which a patient has deteriorated. They are, however, not specifically diagnostic of depression or other problems.

Throughout the evaluation the clinician will wonder: why is this person seeking help now? Have circumstances changed dramatically in the recent past? What has alarmed the patient or family? Through the detailed history the clinician understands what has preceded this visit. The remaining parts of the evaluation will build on what the clinician has learned and will tell more about the present status of the patient.

Mrs. G, in the example above, is able to give a reasonable chronology of her depressive symptoms and their relationship to the events in her life. She denies previous depressions, nor does she think that she has been under undue stress during the past year. She's used to being "in charge of things," and being depressed and dependent is uncomfortable for her. She wonders if it could be physical. She questions whether her metabolism is right. "Maybe this has something to do with the medicine I take for high blood pressure," she says. Her psychologically oriented daughter thinks that Mrs. G is upset because her husband's polyp forced her to confront their vulnerabilities; further, it scared her into thinking that she might actually lose her husband. Or maybe it reflects her anger toward her husband or other significant people in her life. Mrs. G says that she doesn't know what her daughter is talking about. "All I know is that this is very painful, almost physically painful, and I have to get some relief."

The next steps in the work-up are organized to elucidate some of these issues, to answer some of the questions, and clarify the theories that Mrs. G and her daughter have raised.

The Physical Examination

Most clinicians who work with older adults insist on performing a complete physical examination before making a psychological or psychiatric diagnosis and treatment plan. This is usually done by the patient's family physician or internist. Mrs. G wanted to go to her gynecologist, whom she thought of as "her doctor," but her husband persuaded her to seek a more comprehensive evaluation with a family physician. In fact, older adults may visit many physicians in their later years, and the idea that someone is depressed may first occur to the ophthalmologist, urologist, or cardiologist. These doctors may see hints of psychological problem from their contacts with the patient, and refer the patient to more specialized clinicians to further investigate the potential disorder. They should also let the patient, family, and primary care physicians know about their concerns.

Most psychiatrists prefer not to do physical examinations on their patients. They feel that others may be more expert and, in addition, that touching the patient may adversely change the actual or potential psychotherapeutic relationship. Some other psychiatrists, who feel comfortable examining their patients, will not refer to other physicians. Neurologists are an-

other group of specialists who frequently evaluate the elderly
for dementia and/or depression. They are experts in the functioning of the brain and nervous system, and they often work
closely with mental health professionals. If the patient starts
the evaluation with a mental health professional, it is generally
advisable to refer the patient to an internist, family physician,
or neurologist for this part of the assessment. The issues are
often complex and medicine—including psychiatry—is increasingly sophisticated, so having two or more professionals
thinking and talking about the factors involved is quite beneficial. This is a good reason for approaching university-based
clinics or other specialized settings that provide evaluations by
a multidisciplinary team.

The physical examination helps rule out certain diseases that
may start with depression as a primary symptom. These include endocrine disorders, of which thyroid problems are especially apt to cause depression; neurological problems, such
as brain tumors—many of which are treatable if discovered
early; heart failure or chronic lung disorders, which prevent
full oxygenation of the blood; nutritional deficiencies, particularly lack of vitamin B_{12} or folic acid; kidney failures; and
various chronic infections. In fact, almost any disease in the
elderly can first appear with depression.

The physical examination should also focus on the extent to
which an ongoing depression may have weakened a patient
who has been suffering for weeks or months. The patient may
have lost weight because of decreased appetite. In fact, gross
malnutrition may occur in a relatively short time and creates
additional difficulties. Depressed people may not drink enough
fluids and thus may be dehydrated. They generally sleep poorly,
and spend a lot of time in relative inactivity. All of these factors
predispose the depressed person to medical problems and need
to be considered in the physical evaluation.

The physical examination helps to determine how much the
physical complaints of the patient are based on physical illness
and how much they represent a psychosomatic "depressive

equivalent," or hypochondriacal reactions that are part of the depression. Patients may mask their depressive symptoms in new or exaggerated physical symptoms and the extent of this can be clarified in the examination. For these many reasons the physical examination is crucial to any work-up for depression in the elderly, where the mix between mind and body is so apparent.

> Mrs. G's physical examination was normal except for mildly elevated blood pressure and some irregularity of her heartbeat. Her physician speculated that these abnormalities were not related to her depression, and decided to further investigate them with specialized tests.

The Mental Status Examination

The evaluation of mental status is usually best performed by a mental health professional. A geriatric medicine specialist, or an internist or family physician with experience in working with the elderly, can get an accurate picture of the depressed patient through obtaining a history of the problem and performing a physical examination. These physicians are usually the first step in the chain of referrals for problems such as depression. But the psychiatrist or other mental health professional—psychologist, clinical social worker, or psychiatric nurse—is a specialist in these disorders and will usually do a more exhaustive assessment if and when consulted. This specialist evaluation is important for several reasons, including the need to follow a patient over time (sometimes using rather subtle indications of improvement or worsening) and to determine the usefulness and/or side effects of medications or other therapies. The clinician will perform this evaluation by using observations made during discussions with the patient and by asking some very specific questions. Several general areas are focused on during this examination.

The patient's *appearance* is observed from the initial contact and throughout the interview. The extent of the patient's de-

pressed mood is assessed. Is it consistent during the interview
or over several encounters? Is it appropriate to what the patient
is discussing? Does the patient sometimes seem too high spir-
ited? Does he or she make eye contact? Is there evidence of
recent weight gain or loss? What does the patient's body language tell us?

> Mrs. G appeared to be sad, tired, drawn, pale, and slightly
> agitated as she paced in the waiting area, wringing her hands.
> The agitated behavior increased in the consultation room. Mrs.
> G appeared to be slightly disheveled and her dress was stained
> in several places. In contrast to Mrs. G, many depressed pa-
> tients move slowly, a state referred to as "psychomotor retar-
> dation." This improves with treatment as the depression abates.

The *thoughts* of the patient are evaluated in terms of their
content and the *process* of thinking. Clinicians are interested in
knowing what the patient is concerned or preoccupied with,
and whether he or she makes sense in describing those thoughts.
Are the patient's thoughts dominated by past failures, losses,
guilt, sadness, or suicide? How many positive attributes exist
that might sustain the patient in a difficult period or provide
a basis on which to draw in the treatment process? Does the
patient have something to look forward to? Does he or she have
goals? Can the patient appreciate past successes and good times?
Many depressed people forget that there were ever good times.
What does the thought content, as revealed in the interview,
tell about personal strengths and weaknesses? Are there delusions—beliefs that have no basis in reality—such as paranoid
beliefs that someone is stealing valuables from the house or
concerns about the food being poisoned? (Such delusions give
a symbolic hint that the patient is feeling threatened, poor,
vulnerable, or bereft.) Does the patient have hallucinations:
abnormal sensory perceptions that are internally generated,
such as hearing voices that tell the patient how bad he or she
is? The depressed person can get stuck on an idea: obsessed

with a thought that will be repeated often during the interview, and many more times to relatives and friends who will listen. One depressed woman told me no fewer than seven times in the first consultation hour how her mother had died 45 years ago; each time she seemed not to realize that she had already related the story. The story was obviously immensely important to the patient and was crucial to my better understanding the patient. The fact that it preoccupied her was also data that helped me better evaluate her state of mind.

Many depressed elderly people have *thoughts of suicide*, but they must be asked about. It is vital for the clinician to try to understand the extent of a person's preoccupation with suicidal ideas, plans, or acts. No patient first gets suicidal ideas because they are asked about, although some families are shocked to hear that the psychiatrist has inquired. If the psychiatrist is concerned, he or she may want to enlist the family to diminish the risk by ridding the house of potentially lethal weapons, medications, and so on; by providing special watching or nursing while the danger is most acute; or by helping to hospitalize a reluctant or frightened patient for whom hospitalization might offer both protection and treatment.

Mrs. G demonstrated no major thought disorder, and had no evidence of hallucinations or delusions. The content of her thought primarily involved feelings of sadness and some worries—apparently unfounded—about not having enough money to buy food. She had no overt suicidal ideas, although she said that if "this pain of depression" continued she "wouldn't mind being hit by a truck and ending it all." This is a common feeling in depressed people and one that doesn't in itself imply significant suicidal risk. This feeling must be monitored, however, to be certain that changes in circumstances over time, without improvement in mental status, don't cause it to become a more active suicide threat.

The next part of the mental status examination assesses *cognitive functions*. This assessment is particularly important in the older adult because the two major psychiatric problems of late life—depression and dementia—can both affect the individual's ability to think, remember, concentrate, and use information. By accurately evaluating these functions the clinician gets valuable diagnostic clues. Some of the information will be obtained from the patient's responses during the earlier history-taking. Other material will be gained by a systematic review of specific mental functions. It is tempting to base one's assessment on the casual conversation which occurs as part of any interview. The patient may look and sound deceptively healthy until cognitive functions are carefully evaluated.

Clinicians first note whether the patient is "alert"—that is, awake—or whether he or she is in a stupor, or even semicomatose or comatose? If the patient is not alert, an immediate medical examination, usually in the hospital, is required to investigate the possible causes of this altered state of consciousness, called delerium. Even though patients are primarily depressed or demented, they should be alert.

One of the fundamental areas of testing is orientation to person, place, and time. Does the patient know who the people are in his or her environment, where he or she is, and what the time (date, day, etc.) is? These functions are impaired in many elderly people who are relatively isolated, and also in people who are either depressed or demented. Too often this is where nonpsychiatric clinicians start and stop their assessment of mental status. One must further evaluate cognitive functions to get a more complete picture.

Tests of memory may include asking the patient to remember three words or things, to repeat them immediately, and then to repeat them again three or five minutes later. The patient will be asked, in addition, to recall recent news stories, favorite television programs, or family events. Past memory is evaluated in the history-taking and more formally by asking about early schools attended, the names of teachers and friends, the dates of birth of children, the ages of siblings, or the names of recent presidents of the United States starting with the present one.

All of these tests have limitations, in that they have cultural and socioeconomic biases. An experienced clinician will vary the questions to try to use a relevant framework to best assess the patient. Some of the patient's responses may have to be corroborated by a family member.

Concentration may be evaluated by asking the patient to count back by 7s from 100—giving the responses 100, 93, 86, and so on. This, of course, also tests arithmetic ability. A test that is sometimes more acceptable to the patient is spelling a five-letter word backwards (world = d-l-r-o-w). Memory and concentration are tested by having the patient repeat a series of digits forwards and backwards. Abstracting ability is tested by asking for the meanings of various proverbs, such as "No use crying over spilled milk," or "People in glass houses shouldn't throw stones." Another test of abstracting capacity is asking the patient to define the ways in which certain items are similar (e.g., chair and table = furniture) or different.

> Mrs. G was alert and oriented in all ways, although she wasn't sure whether my office was on the fourth or fifth floor. Her past memory was excellent for schools, dates, and names, but she was able to repeat the names of only two test items after five minutes, and said that she was "too nervous" to do serial sevens or to spell a word backwards. That seemed like "a stupid thing to do anyway," she said. With some humor, she noted, "What good is it to spell a word backwards when you need to use it forwards?" She was also quite concrete and personalized in interpreting the proverb, "No use crying over spilled milk," by saying that she "cried a lot over spilled milk"; and that "people in glass houses shouldn't throw stones" because she was afraid that someone would "wreck her house."

The mental status examination is an essential part of the evaluation. The information obtained must be integrated with the other aspects of the assessment so that a more complete clinical picture can be obtained. In the case of Mrs. G, the mental status examination revealed that she had many indications of depression: her appearance was sad, she was agitated and slightly disheveled, her thought content contained many references to depression and poverty, and she personalized the proverbs related to crying and houses (maybe, her life?) "being wrecked." There were also some indications of slight cognitive impairment—incomplete memory and concrete interpretations of abstract proverbs—but these signs were probably the result of depression, rather than some organic brain disorder. To be more certain of the diagnosis, further testing needed to be done.

Laboratory, X-ray, and Other Special Tests

In view of the relationships between depression and other medical conditions, a complete evaluation of the person with symptoms of depression must include a battery of laboratory tests that help rule out medical conditions. In addition, the tests help to assess the extent to which an existing depression may have affected various physical functions. It is important for the patient and family to realize that, although these laboratory studies usually are normal in the depressed person, the small chance that they may yield positive results justifies their use in every situation when they have not been performed in the past six months. One would not want to be treated only for depression when another underlying disease needed attention. The tests are relatively inexpensive, the costs are usually covered by insurance, and they can usually be done from blood drawn from one needle stick or from one urine sample in the doctor's office or hospital laboratory. Most older adults have been to physicians, have had most of these tests done at some point in their lives, and—if they remember—will not be traumatized by them.

The laboratory work-up usually includes:

a complete blood count (CBC);

a urinalysis;

liver and kidney function tests;

a thyroid profile;

electrolyte levels (sodium, potassium, chlorides, etc. in the blood);

a check on levels of vitamin B_{12} and folic acid; and

a blood test for syphilis.

In addition, it is helpful to have a recent chest X-ray and an electrocardiogram (EKG) available for evaluation. An electro-encephalogram (EEG), which measures brain wave activity, may be ordered to check for tumors, strokes, the effects of medications, or metabolic abnormalities. The computerized tomogram (CT scan) has become a valuable tool in diagnosing structural problems within the brain. It is performed during many evaluations for depression, but especially when there appears to be some evidence of neurological deficit or dementia. While the CT scan is useful in locating brain tumors, strokes, and areas of brain damage from some other causes, *it does not specifically indicate whether someone is depressed, nor whether Alzheimer's disease is present*. More sophisticated imaging devices are now being studied that are intended to reveal the structural changes associated with Alzheimer's disease.

Another part of the evaluation for depression may include some standardized "paper and pencil" or questionnaire-type tests. These are usually screening tests, used to get an idea of the presence of depression or dementia and to obtain a numerical score that can be compared with later testing. These tests can be used to measure the effect of treatment or the rate of deterioration of functioning. They can be administered in a clinician's office, often within an hour. Another group of tests are the more comprehensive psychological or neuropsychological batteries, which give some detailed information about the person's thinking processes and may offer some important clues for diagnosis. These tests usually take several hours to administer and can be costly, but when medically indicated these tests are usually reimbursable from health insurances. They are not routinely used by most clinicians, but their use should be discussed more fully with the psychiatrist or other clinician.

All of these procedures may sound like an enormous amount of effort, time, and cost just to determine whether someone is depressed. But it is essential for those in the field of geriatric psychiatry to be as thorough in the evaluation of clinical problems as physicians are when dealing with pneumonia, or heart or kidney disease. Correct diagnosis and treatment is vital no matter what organ system is affected, and when depression is the presenting problem several systems may be involved, so the investigation needs to be as complete as possible. Each part of the examination and each of the blood, urine, X-ray, and other studies yields just one piece of positive or negative information in a puzzle that might include hundreds of parts that the clinicians will evaluate.

What To Do When Someone Won't Get Help

A spouse, adult children, or friends are frequently caught in a bind when they recognize that their loved one shows signs of a psychological problem, possibly depression, and the worrisome person won't do anything about getting help.

Mr. S is a 73-year old electronics specialist who retired from his full-time job at age 68 and has had an active part-time consulting business since then. With his semiretirement he began drinking alcohol to excess, consuming up to a case of beer per week. His wife and children noted that for the past year he had been occasionally disoriented—even when not inebriated—that he had begun to forget the names of business contacts, seemed generally less active in seeking out new business, and systematically turned down invitations for business lunches and other social occasions. He was less careful in his grooming and occasionally forgot to change his shirt after several days of wear. All of these signs were in marked contrast to his behavior in previous years. He now appeared sad and occasionally tearful for no apparent reason. His early morning awakening and decreased appetite were noticed by his wife. He paced in the living room for several hours each day, and usually "barked" at her when she tried to engage him in conversation.

Mr. S's wife approached him about "seeing someone professionally" for his change of behavior and mental state. He angrily retorted that nothing was wrong. She then appealed to her children who, in frustration with their father, went to a psychiatrist for a consultation to try to deal better with him.

The psychiatrist suggested that a medical problem—possibly neurological, possibly psychiatric—might exist, and that a workup to unravel the mystery was in order. Because of the dynamics of the family it was decided that one of Mr. S's daughters and one of his sons would confront their father with their concerns and insist that he get an evaluation to determine the reason for the changes. They prepared for the worst, but surprisingly Mr. S responded to their appeal and made an appointment to see his family physician.

The key factors in helping someone like Mr. S, who was resistant to seeking help, to get an assessment are: 1) firm confrontation, 2) expression of genuine concern, and 3) respect for autonomy. Confrontation is best done by the close relatives or friends who have the most clout with the prospective patient. It should be done by a small group of two to four confronters. Mr. S's wife had been labeled by him as a "nag," and he "was tired of hearing her complain" about his decline. She had lost her credibility with him. Mr. S's son and daughter had seen the changes in their father, but did not live with him and had not been involved with him on a daily basis. Mr. S. had always respected "the sensible ways they conduct their lives" and thought that they had good values. They were the natural confronters, and it required the two of them.

It is useful for the prospective confronters to meet with a mental health professional in advance to think out and organize their ideas and to plan a general approach. It helps that the professional is somewhat removed from the family, but has dealt with these kinds of problems with others. Mr. S's children were encouraged to express their concerns in a supportive way, but to forcefully persuade their father to seek help for what they regarded as a potentially serious problem. They gave Mr. S concrete examples of the ways in which he had declined, and detailed the ways in which they were distressed for him. Respecting his autonomy as a mature adult with a problem, they expected him to follow through with a plan for an evaluation. They offered to assist in the process if he wanted that. They were unyielding against his protests that "everything is under control." Mr. S was still able to see himself as their father, with his two children as partners in this effort. They were able to convey their caring and determination in a firm, supportive manner, which left no doubt in Mr. S's mind that they respected him, were concerned about him, and that they weren't going to be manipulated.

Most resistant older adults welcome this kind of approach. But it isn't always this easy. Unfortunately, a small number of these people will not be persuaded, even by the best prepared, most firm, and most concerned family members. When circumstances change, they may later agree to seek assistance, or the family may have to await further deterioration, when involuntary hospitalization may be the last resort.

In the case of Mr. S, his acceptance of the children's support and confrontation mellowed him, and once his resistance was lowered he was also able to accept his wife as a helping person. At the same time, when her children offered their assistance, Mrs. S felt less alone with the battle, became much less anxious, and was consequently less threatening to her husband. She accompanied him to the physician's office. After a rather exhaustive work-up Mr. S was treated for major depression with medication and psychotherapy. His alcohol intake decreased, he made plans to limit his business involvements, and to finally spend more time in leisure activities.

5

The Diagnoses of Depression

DEPRESSION can be a confusing term. As I have mentioned, many elderly don't use the word, but instead convey the message of distress through various physical, social, and psychological signs and symptoms. But even when the word depression is used, what is meant is sometimes unclear. Is it a feeling, a symptom, or a disorder? In fact, it is all of those, and more.

When older people get depressed it may be a temporary state produced by a bad day, an acute illness, a mourning reaction to a loss, or other factors. They may feel blue or sad, but they may not be particularly disabled; they are able to function in their usual ways, and the sadness doesn't last more than a few days or a week. This kind of depression, or "dysphoria," happens at all ages and doesn't usually prompt a professional consultation unless it is very repetitive. People who are briefly or transiently depressed may talk about their feelings with friends and family, work them out in their own way, or may accept those feelings as part of what it means to be old. Although everyone has some periodic ups and downs, we should be wary of writing off persistent or pervasive sadness or depression as normal, particularly in the elderly, for whom it can have dire consequences.

When I speak about depression in this book I am referring to a set of symptoms—a syndrome or disorder—that is disabling in the sense that it interferes with a usual state of well being or with social or occupational functioning. Inadequate functioning is a subjective term and is often defined by the identified patient or a family member as a change for the worse from past behavior, mood, or functioning, or a failure to live up to some ideal of functioning for which they hope. These personal subjective notions are often what prompts people to get help. Other people are referred by physicians or other professionals because of concern that all is not right or because of multiple or persistent physical complaints. This discussion of diagnosis presumes that all possible physical causes have been ruled out after careful history, physical examination, and appropriate tests have been made by a competent clinician.

Mental health professionals have tried to be increasingly precise in their definitions of diagnoses. To achieve this, they use a rather comprehensive book called the *Diagnostic and Statistical Manual of Mental Disorders* (Washington, D.C.: American Psychiatric Association, 3rd ed., 1980)—often referred to as *DSM III*—which details the criteria for all psychiatric diagnoses. It gives psychiatrists and other mental health clinicians a common language for the many psychiatric problems that afflict their patients, a guide to develop specific treatment criteria for the various diagnoses, a common basis for research into diagnostic categories, and a means to communicate with others, such as insurance companies, who use the definitions to determine insurability and reimbursement. "The diagnosis" assists the clinician in considering what might be the most helpful treatment plan for an individual patient.

In any description of diagnostic criteria we should be aware that we are describing general categories. The variations and mixtures of signs and symptoms are beyond the scope of this book, but can be discussed in any individual case with the clinician involved. Psychiatric diagnostic terms are not "accusations," although many people mistakenly view them as comments on their moral fiber, strength, or character. I prefer to see them in the same light as diagnoses of hypertension, heart disease, or pneumonia. Surely no one sees these as accusations, and few people hesitate to pursue evaluation and treatment of such diseases when symptoms or signs are present.

You may hear psychiatric diagnostic terms used and not know what they mean. Most people outside of the mental health field have this difficulty. I will explain the common diagnoses that are used to describe the problems of depression. These problems are sometimes lumped together as a group and referred to as "affective disorders" or "disorders of mood." They include:

> major depressive episode;
>
> bipolar disorders—manic, depressed, and mixed types;
>
> dysthymic disorder;
>
> abnormal bereavement; and
>
> organic affective syndrome.

Major Depressive Episode

The diagnosis of depression most commonly made by clinicians in older adults is major depressive episode. The criteria, as enumerated by the *DSM III*, include:

> "Dysphoric" mood, characterized by such symptoms as feeling depressed, sad, blue, hopeless, low, down in the dumps, and irritable. These feelings should be prominent and relatively persistent.

> At least four of the following symptoms, present nearly every day for a period of at least two weeks:
>
> 1. Poor appetite or significant weight loss or gain.
>
> 2. Insomnia or oversleeping.

3. Psychomotor agitation or retardation.

4. Loss of interest or pleasure in usual activities.

5. Loss of energy, fatigue, or excessive tiredness.

6. Feelings of worthlessness, self-reproach, or excessive or inappropriate guilt.

7. Complaints or evidence of decreased ability to think or concentrate, such as slowed thinking or indecisiveness.

8. Recurrent thoughts of death, suicide, wishes to be dead, or a suicide attempt.

The DSM III criteria do not take into account the fact that many elderly patients do not complain of being depressed, sad, or blue. In addition, older people often express depression through increased physical symptoms that do not result in a diagnosis of a physical disorder. We must be flexible in our evaluation to include these differences from younger people so we don't miss the depression that may be present.

In the past, major depression has been referred to as "psychotic depression" or "endogenous depression." Those terms imply a serious disorder with probable biological components. Although the depression may be triggered by real or imagined losses or upsets, the extent of the symptoms almost always seems out of proportion to the actual loss. It is as if some internal (endogenous) problem is magnifying the precipitating events, making them seem insurmountable. In spite of its seriousness, major depression is also quite treatable and the vast majority of patients so diagnosed improve or totally recover. (Treatment is discussed in chapter 7.)

Mrs. M is a 79-year-old widowed woman who until one year prior to consultation was a rather independent and high functioning person. She drove her car, played in two weekly bridge games, attended church services, took care of her apartment, and was enrolled in at least one class per week in a local senior center. She had friends with whom she made social engagements and she saw and enjoyed her children and grandchildren.

Approximately eleven months prior to her visit to a geriatric psychiatrist, the carpeting in her apartment was damaged by a burst pipe in the apartment above. The immediate water problem was solved but efforts to prevent staining of her carpet were unsuccessful. The carpeting was 20 years old, was well worn, and was due for replacement soon. Her family thought that she would be happy to know that an insurance company would pay to have her carpet replaced. They were wrong.

Over the next three months Mrs. M became sad, teary, and lethargic. She had difficulty staying asleep at night, had decreased appetite, lost ten pounds, and seemed to lose interest in most of the activities she had enjoyed before. She didn't want to spend any time at home in her apartment, choosing to visit friends, sit in restaurants alone, or ask a friend to take her somewhere—anywhere. She stopped reading and complained that she couldn't concentrate on anything.

Mrs. M became obsessed with the damage to her carpet and procrastinated when the family made efforts to help her pick out new carpeting. She talked freely, saying that her life was over anyway, so why should she get new carpeting, even though it was free?

After six months of symptoms Mrs. M agreed, at her daughter's urging, to see a psychiatrist for consultation, although she said that she didn't believe in psychiatry. Her depressive symptoms were vastly out of proportion to her real loss. The carpet served as a focus for her depressed feelings. Something had been stirred up by the carpet event. She was unable to deal with efforts to put the episode in perspective, and brief "talking therapy" attempted to focus on her many previous losses and disappointments. She was able to reminisce about the good and bad times in her life and to cry about some things that she said she hadn't talked about in 20 or 25 years. (Those "things" were as old as her carpet.) She was also treated with antidepressant medications to which she responded dramatically over the first three weeks of therapy.

She gradually resumed her activities, managed to pick out some new carpeting just prior to the insurance company's deadline, and seemed to be increasingly content. Six months later she was "back to normal," and she had difficulty remembering that she had been so upset in the recent past. She decided to stop seeing the psychiatrist.

Mrs. M suffered with symptoms of a major depressive episode for approximately six months before seeking help. Her symptoms included sadness, teariness, fatigue, insomnia, loss of appetite with weight loss, loss of interest and pleasure in activities, indecisiveness, and feelings of worthlessness. They represented a radical change in behavior and state of mind from her previous high level of functioning. Although she didn't "believe in psychiatry," she fully participated and responded well to treatment.

Bipolar Disorder

Bipolar affective disorders, previously known as "manic–depressive illness," are less common than major depression, but they must not be overlooked in the elderly. Bipolar disorders commonly arise in early or middle adulthood and may persist into late life. In some situations, however, the very first episode appears in the elderly adult. "Bipolar" typically implies both manic and depressive episodes, which occur in alternating or periodic fashion and last days, weeks, or months, with or without level periods. Whether manic or depressive episodes predominate, there is usually a history of the other state somewhere in the patient's past.

Manic symptoms include elation or euphoria, hyperactivity, decreased need for sleep, agitation, irritability, grandiosity, pressured speech, or flight of ideas. Many of these manic symptoms appear to be the opposite of depression and, indeed, many of them are experienced as pleasurable by the affected patient. The symptom complex is nonetheless pathological because it is disabling, results in poor judgment, impulsiveness, and erratic behavior and thinking. The complex seems to be a variant of the same biological and psychodynamic issues that produce true depression.

An 82-year-old semiretired businessman who owned a large corporation with 200 employees came to a geriatric clinic at the urging of his daughters because of persistent agitation and an inability to sleep for more than three hours per night. He would awaken and call his daughters in the middle of the night with rather inconsequential questions "that had to be answered immediately." He had difficulty sticking to an idea or thought without "jumping all over the place," and seemed to have boundless energy. He was not elated, but rather was irritable, and he verbalized intermittent paranoid ideas that there was a conspiracy against him and his business. Although generally astute in his business dealings, he now often left important matters unattended. Three months prior to the consultation he impulsively spent $15,000 on a new car and contracted to buy a new house. He was living well beyond his means and had approached a local bank about a $25,000 loan. He had a history of many episodes of "deep depression" over the past thirty years, and had been treated previously with medications of various types, electroshock therapy, and stimulants. He had had infrequent "excited" episodes only in the recent past. At those times he refused the recommended treatment of lithium, because he felt "too good." Two of his cousins had histories of "nervous breakdowns" many years ago and both had died in mental hospitals.

At the time of the mental status examination, this gentleman was flamboyantly dressed in plaid golf pants, a print shirt, and a colorful tie; he looked younger than his 82 years. He was gregarious, a bit loud, and seemed unable to stop talking. He could not concentrate on the tasks of the interview and could not remain seated in the office, wondering whether the room was "bugged." He demonstrated "flight of ideas" and the content of his thoughts was difficult to follow. He had a good sense of humor, and appeared to be a bright man, with no evidence of gaps in his thinking ability. He rejected the idea that he needed help and had no recollection of being depressed in the past. With some convincing by his family he agreed to enter the hospital for "some tests." He later also agreed to a treatment program that included medications and that helped to greatly diminish his symptoms.

People with bipolar illness are more likely to have a family history of affective disorders, are more likely to have problems with alcohol abuse (sometimes in an effort to control the manic symptoms or to sleep), and are at greater risk of suicide than are people with depressive episodes alone. Bipolar illness is highly responsive to treatment with lithium and/or tranquilizing medications (to be discussed in chapter 7). Depending on the predominant symptoms, bipolar disorders are classified as manic, depressed, or mixed (both), although both symptoms are usually present at some point in the course of the illness. Many bipolar patients seem to have little or no recollection of the depressed periods when they are manic and little recall of better times when they are depressed. That fact sometimes complicates their motivations for treatment, as they often have difficulty seeing the problem as a chronic one.

Dysthymic Disorder

This diagnosis was previously commonly referred to as "depressive neurosis," a term still used by many mental health professionals. Although popularized, the term "neurosis" has been used since Freud's day and included a group of symptoms thought to have arisen because of early childhood traumas. The characteristic feature of dysthymic disorders is a chronic mood disturbance in which there is a generalized loss of pleasure and interest in almost all usual life activities; however, the disturbance is not sufficiently severe or does not have the necessary elements to qualify as a major depressive episode. People with dysthymic disorders do not have the vegetative symptoms of appetite and sleep disturbances, weight loss, and physical complaints. Dysthymic disorder usually begins early in adult life without a clear time of onset. The specific criteria, as outlined in the *DSM III*, include:

Depressive symptoms over the past two years that are not as severe as those for a major depressive episode.

Depressive symptoms that are persistent; when remitted, there are normal periods of only days or weeks.

During the depressive episodes, at least three of the following symptoms exist:

1. Insomnia or hypersomnia.
2. Low energy or chronic tiredness.
3. Feelings of inadequacy, low self-esteem, or self-depreciation.
4. Decreased effectiveness or productivity.
5. Decreased attention, concentration, or ability to think clearly.
6. Social withdrawal.
7. Loss of interest in pleasurable activities.
8. Irritability or excessive anger.
9. Cannot respond with pleasure to praise or rewards.
10. Less active or talkative than usual, or feels slowed down or restless.
11. Pessimistic attitude toward the future, brooding about past events, or feeling sorry for self.
12. Tearfulness or crying.
13. Recurrent thoughts of death or suicide.

Absence of psychotic features, such as delusions or hallucinations.

The layman may have difficulty seeing the distinctions in these diagnoses. In fact, there may be some blurring at the extremes of the syndromes. Dysthymic disorder generally implies a chronic, less-severe problem than a major depressive episode or bipolar disorder. Nonetheless, the patient may feel or, in fact, be quite disabled and in need of treatment. Some clinicians prefer to think of depression as extending on a continuum from mild to severe, with the latter group usually including the symptoms described for the major depressive episode and the milder group comprising the dysthymic disorders. Dysthymic disorders are sometimes life-long problems, which may be exaggerated by life events such as deaths, illness, and losses.

Mrs. P is a 72-year-old widowed woman who sought help because of long-standing feelings of inadequacy and low self-esteem and more immediate feelings of depression and anxiety. While she recognized that these feelings had probably existed for many years, they became more "depressing" to her following the recent deaths of two close friends on whom she had depended for over 10 years. In the past two years she had symptoms of sadness, insomnia, decreased interest in socializing, irritability, and occasional tearfulness. She preferred to spend time in the lobby of her apartment building because she felt insecure in her own apartment. Although Mrs. P generally felt "down" and pessimistic about her life, she admitted that she was able to spend some good time with her family and still liked talking with some of her old friends. She enjoyed it when her children and grandchildren took her out for lunches and dinner, but she felt that they didn't visit her often enough.

Mrs. P was physically healthy. She took no medications except for occasional tranquilizers. She walked in her neighborhood every day, although she recently only walked around the block because she got tired so easily. Although she participated in some social activities, she was always "revved up" from the time the plans were made until the event was over. She had no hallucinations, delusions, or suicidal ideas.

During the mental status examination, Mrs. P related in a sad, occasionally tearful, pleasant but rather whiney, dependent manner. The content of her thought primarily concerned her need for care-taking, her loneliness, and her inability to enjoy much. She was fully competent cognitively and demonstrated some insight into her long-standing inadequacies, the more recent anxiety and depressive symptoms, and their relationship to her unmet dependency needs.

Mrs. P had been treated with a minor tranquilizer for what her physician thought was "chronic anxiety." Although it made her feel less nervous, it also made her more depressed, she thought. Under the supervision of her new psychiatrist, who diagnosed dysthymic disorder, Mrs. P's dose of the minor tranquilizer was tapered until it was discontinued, and then she began an antidepressant medication. She also was seen weekly for supportive psychotherapy, which focused on her personal strengths, sociability, family ties, and her use of walking as an outlet. She slowly felt better, although after three months she only would admit to being "improved but not cured."

Bereavement: Normal and Abnormal

Mrs. K is a 74-year-old woman whose husband died of lung cancer after two years of illness. They had been married for 55 years. After his death she realized that she had been "pampered, treated like a queen" by him for all those years. And now her "king" was dead. In fact, Mrs. K found that she was very lonely, did not know how things worked around the house—except in the kitchen—and had no concept of how to manage even the day-to-day finances. She realized that she never shopped for clothes without him, never made a decision without his advice, and never even planned a dinner menu without checking with him in advance—for fifty-five years!

When seen in the geriatric psychiatry clinic 13 months after her husband's death, she was tearful when talking about him and about her current status. She emphasized her inability to do anything, her lack of pleasure in any activity, her repetitive dreams that he was lying next to her in the bed, and her occasional idea that he was "just out for a walk." She thought about the prospect of "joining him," but did not have suicidal thoughts.

What is normal grief after a long marriage? Clinicians expect that after the death of a close relative it takes up to several years to grieve the loss, to regain full function, or to begin to set up a new life that is relatively independent of the dead spouse or other relative. In that time there may be sleeplessness, decreased appetite, loss of interest or enjoyment in activities, a taking on of attributes or habits of the deceased person, and guilt over what was done or not done by the survivor. These symptoms are common in the first six months to one year and generally resolve over the next year. But there may be complications.

Abnormal grief reactions may have many of the symptoms characteristic of a major depression: increases in physical or psychosomatic symptoms; agitation; withdrawal from relationships with significant people; thoughts of worthlessness, hopelessness, and helplessness; suicidal thoughts; cognitive deterioration; near total preoccupation with the loss; and the reactivation of the experiences of past losses. Even previously competent people may appear to have "regressed." They may refuse to eat, and may act in childish, defiant, or manipulative ways that increasingly frustrate and eventually infuriate other family members who are also struggling with the recent loss.

After 55 years in a rather dependent relationship, Mrs. K surely feels not only alone but totally inept. Some people in this state are inconsolable and grieve for virtually the rest of their lives. Others, profoundly affected, die within six months or a year after the death of a spouse, literally unable to survive alone. These reactions are clearly pathological, and as signs of abnormal grief appear, professional consultation should be sought. A surviving spouse is at high risk for severe depression and even for physical illness in the months immediately following the death. Some mental health professionals advocate preventive counseling for the elderly surviving spouse in the period immediately after the death.

Why the abnormal reactions? Sometimes they are the expression of real helplessness, as experienced by Mrs. K. Because she was a very sheltered child and adolescent, she may have chosen a husband who continued that pattern. After his death, Mrs. K, at an advanced age, had to learn some skills of daily living that most people learn in adolescence and young adulthood.

In many grief reactions ambivalent feelings about the deceased complicate the mourning. Most of us have some mixed feelings about everyone, even our most loved ones. The stress of the illness and death of a spouse or child may arouse or exaggerate negative feelings such as anger that are difficult for most people to confront, especially after a death. The anger may concern the recent past or may be a summation of dashed dreams and unrealized expectations—which are now even further from realization. These unacceptable feelings may fester to become the seeds of a more serious depression in the survivor.

It is difficult to say exactly when normal grief becomes abnormal. What is acceptable varies with different cultures and families and has to be tempered by the length and nature of the relationship. Many cultures and religions accept a year of mourning, but after 55 years of marriage most people need longer to grieve. We judge the mourning process as pathological by the presence of symptoms as well as by length of time. Symptoms of major depression after six months, or a suicidal preoccupation at any time are causes for concern and indicate a need for professional attention. But even "normal" people think about their losses daily, become teary and briefly distressed on occasion for years, and sometimes for the rest of their lives. They are, however, generally able to enjoy their lives, feel and be productive, and resume what was their previous level of social functioning.

Organic Affective Syndrome

When used for a psychiatric diagnosis, the term "organic" implies a temporary or permanent brain dysfunction caused by such disorders as a stroke, Alzheimer's disease, toxic and medication reactions, and physical illness in other parts of the body. These "insults" to the brain may cause actual brain damage or temporary disruption of the brain function. They result in behavioral or psychological abnormalities that may resemble some of the diagnoses I have written about above.

An organic affective syndrome is a mood disorder typified by a manic episode or major depressive episode that results from some specific organic problem with the brain. The symptoms very much resemble those detailed for the manic and depressive episodes. It is crucial for the clinician to consider this rare diagnosis because the possible effects on the brain may be reversible if diagnosed and treated early.

Diagnosing depressions within these specific categories may seem like an intellectual exercise. It is much more than that. The process of diagnosis forces the clinician to categorize the signs and symptoms gathered from the history and the physical and mental status examinations. The clinician tries to fill in missing information from other sources and to formulate a plan for treatment that is based on experience with others with similar problems and the accumulated clinical and research knowledge base. The patient and the family benefit from this process, but are understandably mostly interested in what the treatment will be, whether it will work, and when will it take effect. The treatments for depression vary with the severity of the symptoms and the nature of the specific diagnosis. These are subjects I will explore in chapter 7.

6

Dementia: What Is It?
What Is Its Relationship
to Depression?

Mr. H is a 68-year-old man who was brought to a geriatric psychiatry clinic by his wife because of increasing inability to remember the names of common household items and, more strikingly, the names of his grandchildren. This progressive forgetfulness had begun about two years previously, when he rather impulsively decided to seek early retirement from his high-level technical position. When questioned more closely, Mrs. H realized that her husband probably had begun to forget technical details related to his work several years earlier. He became less interested in tuning up his car and seemed to be neglectful of it and the other machinery with which he had previously loved to tinker. He seemed a little depressed at times. The family became alarmed when he received a letter from his sister and didn't know who she was. They were referred to a geriatric psychiatry clinic by their family for evaluation and diagnosis.

THE term "dementia" means the loss of brain function and refers to a set of symptoms that are usually produced by structural changes in the brain. With time these changes result in a gradual but persistent deterioration of neurological and psychological functioning. Typical findings in a patient with dementia include memory impairment, loss of concentration, disorientation, loss of intellectual functioning, and in the late stages, loss of ability to perform activities of daily living such as dressing, toileting, and feeding oneself.

Alzheimer's disease, the most common form of dementia, is a disorder that results in the progressive deterioration of the neurons of the brain. Over the past five years the media has focused a great deal of publicity on Alzheimer's disease. The scientific community has also become increasingly interested in finding out more about what causes this catastrophic illness of middle to late life. In spite of the wealth of publicity about it, however, Alzheimer's disease is still quite misunderstood by lay and professional people.

Although most elderly adults are healthy and grow old without significant impairment, Alzheimer's disease is a monumental problem. Alzheimer's disease affects approximately 5 to 10 percent of the population over 65 years of age. It may affect 20 percent of the population over 80 years. Alzheimer's disease is progressive: its symptoms increase in number and severity in the months and years after onset, resulting in death in 5 to 15 years (the average is 7–8 years). At this point there is no specific treatment of Alzheimer's disease; however, many of the associated symptoms can be eased with medications and psychotherapy, the remaining functions can be maximized, and the patient and family members can be counseled and supported through the difficult times ahead.

Alzheimer's disease was first described in 1907 and it was thought to be a brain failure that occurred in the presenile age group—typically people in their 40s and 50s. In the late 1960s it was discovered that the specific pathological changes in the brains of middle-aged patients who died of Alzheimer's disease were also present in older adults dying of "senility." This finding, verified by several investigators, had significant implications. It meant that senility was not necessarily the inevitable end of the life cycle, but was, in fact, a disease that probably had a cause or several causes and possibly could be treated or prevented. It also meant that Alzheimer's disease was not a rare presenile problem, but was, instead, a major cause of senility and an enormous public health issue that needed to be addressed in view of a rapidly growing elderly population. It was in this light that scientific research and public attention in the 1970s and 1980s focused on the problem of Alzheimer's disease as a major cause of dementia in the aged. Some things have been learned; much more remains to be discovered.

The Symptoms of Alzheimer's Disease

Increasing forgetfulness is usually the first symptom of Alzheimer's disease. It is also a common complaint of *normal* middle-aged and older adults who *do not go on to develop Alzheimer's disease*, but rather have a self-limited "benign senescent forgetfulness." For those with early Alzheimer's disease there is a progressive memory deficit, with increasing difficulty recalling words and names. The early signs are often subtle and only with very detailed questioning of the patient, spouse, or other relatives does the early course of the illness become clear. People at this stage usually try to cover up their deficits in social and occupational situations. They are embarrassed and frightened about what is happening to them. At the next stage of the disease, memory impairment, decreased vocabulary, and difficulty with concentration limit effectiveness in work and social settings. Patients go on to have other problems, such as the inability to find new places around the community, but they are able to follow routine patterns, such as familiar walking routes. They may be unable to handle money responsibly. They are increasingly aware of their deficits and may become depressed at seeing their impairments becoming more evident. They therefore strive to avoid situations that tax their deteriorating mental capacity.

Mr. H clearly was in this stage at the time of referral. As the disease progressed he forgot the names of colors and was unable to find his way around his rather modest house. He clung to the idea that he remembered his home town, but on a trip there he became very disoriented and was upset that he could not find his way to formerly familiar places. He was unable to drive his car, although he very much wanted to do so. He was able to remain at home with his wife and a part-time housekeeper, but needed to be supervised in virtually all activities. He became increasingly dependent on his wife and didn't want her to leave his sight, becoming very agitated whenever she left the house. Great strides were made when he agreed to participate in a senior day program for people with Alzheimer's and related diseases.

Mr. H soon had trouble using eating utensils and wasn't sure what the different foods on his plate were. He continued to enjoy music and remembered how to play simple melodies on the piano.

In the next phase of the disease, patients become increasingly physically and mentally disabled, and require assistance with even the most routine tasks, including picking out clothing, dressing, and bathing. They may fail to recognize their own spouses, referring to them by other names or developing delusions that they are imposters. The patients may become significantly agitated, even violent at times.

In the last stages of Alzheimer's disease the patients are usually disoriented, very confused, and grossly incapacitated. They forget their own identities—names, former occupations, and so on. They may require nursing care as they become incontinent and lose the ability to speak. They may develop an array of other disabling neurological and psychiatric symptoms that render them nonfunctional. Death occurs, often mercifully, because of infection. All patients are different in the way the disease progresses: some faster, some slower, and with very variable symptom complexes. Although this illness is truly catastrophic and leaves the patient increasingly disabled and the family often devastated, frustrated, and exhausted, there are ways in which medical and social service personnel can be of assistance.

Other Dementias

Although Alzheimer's disease is the most common dementia, several other related conditions are prevalent. "Multi-infarct dementia" is caused by many small strokes that gradually produce a loss of brain tissue due to insufficient circulation to the affected areas of the brain. It is associated with hypertension and usually progresses in a step-wise pattern of symptoms, often with long periods of stable functioning. Multi-infarct dementia may not produce inevitable deterioration if the strokes are recognized and can be prevented. In the past multi-infarct dementia has been referred to as hardening of the arteries. We now know that arteries probably can't get "hard enough" to cause dementia, although the arteriosclerosis that is implied by the term hardening of the arteries certainly can cause a number of other physical problems because of the poor circulation that occurs. Patients with Parkinson's disease and Huntington's chorea may also have dementia in the later stages of those disorders.

An important group of dementias, perhaps accounting for up to 20 percent of the cases of dementia, are potentially reversible. Because of this, it is negligent to assign the irreversible status of Alzheimer's disease to every patient with symptoms of dementia. The reversible or treatable dementias also present the symptoms of brain failure, but the *causes* of those symptoms include the adverse effects of certain medications, depression, metabolic and endocrine problems (thyroid abnormalities), certain nutritional abnormalities, and neurological conditions. Just as patients with depression need to be thoroughly worked-up for other medical conditions, so patients with dementia require the same kind of attentive investigation to make an accurate diagnosis. Clinicians must guard against thinking that every patient with dementia has an incurable illness. Up to 20 percent of dementia may be reversible. Patients and family members should insist on a complete evaluation. They should also never tolerate the notion that the symptoms of dementia are a normal part of growing old.

Mr. P is a 69-year-old semiretired lawyer who was found wandering around in the snow, muttering something about his dog. He was disoriented, unable to remember his address, and seemed relatively uninformed. He was stopped by the police and taken to a community hospital where he was evaluated. His medical, neurological, and psychiatric examinations had shown no evidence of a specific cause of the dementia, so the presumptive diagnosis was Alzheimer's disease. He became agitated when told that he needed to be in a nursing home, and a major tranquilizer was added to an extensive regimen of drugs necessitated by several long-standing cardiac and metabolic problems.

Mr. P had no immediate family, but a niece visiting from a distant city was shocked to see her uncle's condition, just six months after he had argued a major case in court. She questioned the diagnosis. A consultant was approached to review the case and found that Mr. P had not been tried off his medications or at reduced doses while being evaluated. Furthermore, three months prior to Mr. P's mental deterioration a new medication for a heart rhythm disturbance had been added.

When the latter medication was tapered, Mr. P's dementia remitted. The diagnosis of Alzheimer's disease had been incorrect. Mr. P suffered from an uncommon toxic effect of a medication that he could not tolerate, even though it had been properly prescribed in therapeutic doses.

Although this case is unusual, it is not rare. Medications and some medical illnesses can precipitate dementia-like symptoms just as they can precipitate depressive symptoms. This kind of treatable, reversible dementia has to be distinguished from Alzheimer's disease in the course of an evaluation.

Making the Diagnosis

In most cases of dementia the family members are usually enormously relieved to have found a diagnostic team that can answer their nagging fears that something is dreadfully and progressively wrong with their friend, parent, or spouse. Even if the "answer" is the diagnosis of an as-yet-incurable illness, they seem willing to try to cope with what is now known, with some hope that in the lifetime of their loved one, better answers will arise.

The first thing that can be done is to get an accurate diagnosis after a work-up similar to the one detailed for depression. No one test gives a positive diagnosis of Alzheimer's disease, though active efforts are being made to discover a method for early diagnosis. Through a complete medical/psychiatric/neurological work-up clinicians attempt to rule out the treatable forms of dementia before dealing with an incurable illness such as Alzheimer's disease. In Alzheimer's disease as in any catastrophic illness there is an understandable tendency for the family to seek repeated medical opinions. After an evaluation by a recognized specialist or a specialty clinic it is a good time for a family to stop shopping around for another doctor who will tell them something more pleasant. A diagnosis can be relieving to a family, although there may be a long period of grieving as the reality hits home. Then what?

Treatment

In our clinic, attention is directed to the identified patient and to the family—often separately, sometimes together. Patients with dementia often benefit from psychotherapy to help them deal with the loss of function they experience and the sadness that it produces. Working with a patient in the early stages of Alzheimer's disease raises the question of what to tell him or her about the disease, course, and prognosis. This, of course, has to be decided on an individual basis and with some family consultation, but it generally seems appropriate to let the patient know that the memory problem will probably get worse and will become an increasing burden. Both family members and the patient need to take financial and legal steps to safeguard family assets. The family and the patient need continuing care, support, and guidance to deal with the progressive stages of this disease. Support groups in the community, family meetings, and whatever usual supports the family uses in times of crisis need to be mustered. A mental health professional can often help facilitate that effort. There are now several excellent family guides, and one should be read by family care-givers. The primary care-giver, usually a spouse or child, needs permission and a system to be periodically relieved of the emotional and physical strain of caretaking. He or she must have support and help in finding ways to deal with the pain, losses, and burdens inherent in the illness of a loved one. Most important, the care-giver must be encouraged not to feel guilty about continuing the enjoyable aspects of his or her life and about maintaining a family and outside social life.

The patient may require medication to deal with agitation, delusions, severe depression, or other symptoms. Major and minor tranquilizers, antidepressants, and sedatives are all potentially useful for symptomatic relief. In addition, a group of drugs called memory enhancers may in some cases slow the progress of the memory loss. These medications are generally safe, although their effectiveness is controversial.

Although they will progressively lose function, many people with Alzheimer's disease can live happily at home and enjoy their families, friends, and environment for many years before the most disabling symptoms occur.

Much research is in progress at institutions all over the world, and families can stay aware of developments in the field through reports in the media and via the Alzheimer's Disease and Related Disorders Association (ADRDA), which has local units across the United States. Because of the immense amount of research now being conducted in the area of early diagnosis, causes, and possible treatments, there is some hope that in the near future we will know much more about Alzheimer's disease, its course, and specific treatments than we now do.

The "reversible" dementias are treatable to the extent that the underlying disease causing the dementia can be treated. For example, if a patient has symptoms of dementia because of an underactive thyroid gland, adding thyroid hormone may well cure the dementia; in a patient with dementia symptoms caused by depression, treatment with medications and psychotherapy directed at the depressive symptoms will cause the dementia to remit. One of the most common causes of reversible dementia is the adverse effect of medications, as in the case of Mr. P. Discontinuing the medication causing those symptoms will reverse the dementia. Because of the dramatic improvements that can result from the treatment of this group of dementias, it is of the utmost importance that they be specifically considered before a diagnosis of Alzheimer's disease or one of the other as-yet-incurable dementias is made.

Depression and Alzheimer's Disease

What does depression have to do with Alzheimer's disease? Depression may be a secondary symptom in patients with Alzheimer's disease or some other form of dementia (i.e., multi-infarct dementia). It is depressing to realize that you are losing mental functioning and gradually becoming increasingly disabled intellectually, psychologically, and neurologically. It is depressing to have increasing difficulty in remembering the names of things that used to be familiar and of people whom you knew well. In addition, it is possible that the deterioration of the neurons in the brain produces a biological or organic depression that is quite separate in origin from the reactive depression described previously. Many patients in the early and middle stages of a progressive dementia are quite depressed as they witness their own deterioration. Although they may continue to lose cognitive function, treating the depressive symptoms enhances the quality of their lives and also maximizes their remaining mental abilities. The depression then no longer exists as a complication of the dementia.

As I have previously noted, depression is sometimes confused with Alzheimer's disease in patients who have no organic brain disorder. When a major depressive episode includes the cognitive symptoms of disturbances in thinking, memory, and concentration, the diagnosis of depression is sometimes not thought of and therefore not treated. The condition is assumed to be Alzheimer's disease. When treatment is initiated and is successful, the symptoms of the cognitive dysfunction in these patients improve as the depression abates.

7

The Treatment

D EPRESSION is one of the most treatable medical problems known and also one of the most common. Ironically, it most often goes untreated. We seek consultations for ourselves, and we take our loved ones to doctor after doctor to get second and third opinions about disorders of the heart, kidneys, bowels, and every other organ system. But somehow we often don't think of depression as a real problem or one that has real treatments. Untreated depression is one of the most painful illnesses of any age, with possibly dire consequences: a life of darkness, feelings of doom, increased medical illness, and even death. Depression that is treated properly can add years of productivity and happiness to someone who had given up hope for those aspects of life.

The treatment of any psychiatric and any medical problem begins with the initial inquiry or contact. I have divided evaluation and treatment into separate chapters for descriptive purposes, but in fact one usually closely follows the other, often in the same setting or even with the same clinician. That's not to say there aren't problems proceeding from one to the other. Although older adults are generally willing to go for some tests—even extensive tests—embarking on a regimen of therapy, whether talking psychotherapy or medication, frequently meets with significant resistance. The patient requires the support, often persuasion, and sometimes even the threats of the family, as well as the encouragement and conviction of the therapists who are consulted.

The present generation of older adults thinks of mental health professionals, particularly psychiatrists, as treating "crazy" people. "Surely I don't need someone like that. I'm not crazy. I'd be taking up their valuable time. They could be treating someone who really needs it." This is a common refrain. I suspect that future generations of elderly will more easily accept the significance of psychological issues in their lives and treatment may be more acceptable to obtain. Increasing numbers of people, however, *do* see the possibility that treatment may be helpful and readily accept the prospect, either because they are in great pain and are desperate or because they have a somewhat more enlightened view of the psychological aspects of life. Most people are frightened of the prospect of seeking treatment for a psychiatric problem and may worry about being regarded as "crazy" or "being put away" somewhere. Common fears such as these can be anticipated and addressed by family members and professional personnel.

What does "treatment" or "therapy" mean? Is it a lifelong commitment? Are the medications dangerous? Does "talk therapy" really work? Isn't electroshock therapy dangerous and barbaric? Should treatment be done in an office, or does mom or dad or Aunt Edith have to go into the hospital? These questions are commonly asked and are concerns to any patient or family member seeking help for depression. This section gives you an overview of possible treatment plans and answers those common questions. Patients and family members should ask their individual questions of the clinicians working with them and get reasonable answers. Although it is usually difficult to make an exact prognosis, an expert therapist can tell you what his or her experience has been with the kind of problem you are having and what the pros and cons may be to various treatment options. Psychiatry is not mystical nor mysterious. It is increasingly scientific. In making effective treatment plans, all clinicians now draw on a significant and growing body of research concerning the treatment of affective disorders. Depression in the elderly can be disabling and life-threatening—sensible and vigorous treatment is mandatory!

What are the treatment options? There are probably dozens of possibilities, but some are more commonly used alone or in combination. These include:

psychotherapy ("talk therapy") of various kinds,

medications, and

electroconvulsive ("shock") therapy.

Psychotherapy

Psychotherapy is a general term for "talk therapy" and includes a variety of techniques with different theoretical bases. Many patients say, "If it's just talk I can do that with my friends or with the bridge group. They understand me and they have similar problems." For minor or temporary upsets talking with friends can be very useful. Many difficulties have been solved and much "psychotherapy" has been done at the card table. However, the advantage of talking with a trained psychotherapist is that he or she is objective and not personally involved. This allows the therapist to help the patient identify themes and patterns in behavior, thoughts, and feelings that people closer to the scene may not see.

Classical psychotherapy is described as "dynamic" or "psychoanalytic" and had its origins in Sigmund Freud's work in the early to middle 1900s. Although Freud was not optimistic that older adults have the capacity to change through psychotherapy, several of his disciples recommended intensive psychotherapy as a treatment for the elderly and found it successful. Dynamic or psychoanalytic psychotherapy involves the patient saying "what's on his mind" and, to the extent possible, expressing thoughts and feelings in as uncensored a manner as is possible. The therapist or analyst remains neutral and objective, and helps the patient to understand the anxieties, conflicts, and pain inherent in the depression. Implicit in psychoanalytic theory is that early childhood experiences and traumas play a large role in later dysfunction. The therapist relies on the patient's memories, dreams, free associations, and the feelings that develop between patient and therapist ("the transference") to understand the patient's problems. By interpreting those understandings to the patient, the therapist can elicit insights and eventually changes in thinking, feeling, or behavior. This technique sounds a bit mysterious, inefficient, and haphazard, but it often produces changes and has been useful as a technique for many people.

The psychoanalytic technique is often not selected by older adults because it requires years rather than months of therapy, it can be expensive, and usually it is applicable alone only for people with mild to moderate depression. It is generally not recommended as the sole treatment for older adults with major depressive episodes where there are expressions of hopelessness, worthlessness, sleep changes, weight loss, and suicidal thoughts. Many elderly people feel the press of time and want to get on with their lives with little delay. They see extensive therapy as stalling. Some others want to keep down what has long been covered up and don't want a therapy in which old feelings and thoughts will be explored. However, some elderly people see psychoanalytic therapy as an intellectual and/or psychological opportunity to explore the past and better understand the present. They avidly participate in the therapy and gain from the experience.

For older adult patients with moderate to severe depression, diagnosed with either a major depressive episode or bipolar disorder, I recommend and primarily use a combination of psychotherapy and medication. The psychotherapy uses some of the principles of the dynamic approach and some principles of "supportive" psychotherapy. "Dynamic" implies the understanding of why and how people feel and think about themselves and their relationships, both in the past and present.

"Supportive" implies the acknowledgment of strengths and useful defenses that have served the patient well in the past and can be mobilized and increased to master a difficult situation or painful time of life. It is neither necessary nor desirable for everyone to delve into all aspects of the past and understand all the psychological details of one's early childhood. This issue will be weighed by the therapist and considered with the patient during the evaluation.

It is important for people with psychological pain to talk. Although talking may not always be curative by itself, it is almost always relieving. The older adult has a wealth of experiences that demonstrate strengths and weakness, recurrent themes and new concerns. The therapy can utilize reminiscence techniques, in which patients are encouraged to review their life experiences to draw on assets that may have been overlooked and to come to terms with difficult issues that may not have been worked through in the past. The therapy must focus on a range of considerations from early childhood worries to the real dilemmas, problems, and exaggerations of old age. Depressed older adults can well use the support offered by an empathic therapist who attempts to build on the defenses that work well for the patient. The therapist can convey an optimistic view that the psychological problem is treatable. He or she can help the patient understand the course of the disorder and recognize the changes that result from treatment. Sessions may be scheduled once or twice per week, with each session lasting thirty to fifty minutes. This approach to treatment requires a flexible therapist who understands the dynamics of normal aging and the complications that depression brings to it.

Psychotherapy that entails this comprehensive approach, combined with medication, produces considerable relief in weeks to months. Up to 75 percent of patients get good results. Some people decide to continue in therapy after the most distressing symptoms are relieved in order to resolve life issues that are more chronically troubling or to continue to benefit from the support that psychotherapy offers. Others stop and may later return for brief periods at times of particular stress or crisis. Patients who do well on medication alone will need only infrequent visits to the psychiatrist or other physician who prescribes the treatment. These visits allow time to evaluate for continuing need, to watch for possible toxic effects, to make dosage adjustments, and to deal with occasional crises.

Other Forms of Psychotherapy

In addition to dynamic and supportive techniques, other popular and effective individual treatments include cognitive and behavior therapies. These are time-limited or short-term approaches that focus on the here and now.

Cognitive therapy helps patients to look at the negative thoughts they have about themselves and the world around them. It attempts to correct thinking habits that perpetuate their negative views. The therapist uses logic and persuasion to correct the patient's view of reality. Cognitive therapy has been effective in treating people with mild to moderate depression, but should not be used alone with major depressive or manic episodes.

Behavior therapy attempts to change dysfunctional behaviors in depressed patients and pays little attention to thoughts or feelings. Patients or family members are encouraged to list behaviors that are symptomatic of or associated with the depression, and a regimen is devised to gain mastery over those behaviors. Techniques such as desensitization, positive reinforcement, assertiveness, and relaxation training are used. The therapist functions as a trainer or coach to effect the change. This approach has been used in hospital and out-patient settings and appeals to many patients who can follow the rather structured guidelines it offers.

Group psychotherapy can use any of the techniques previously mentioned and also includes socialization, activity-oriented, and educative approaches. Group therapists may use any combination of these techniques. Although many patients fear sharing their feelings, thoughts, and behaviors with strangers, that obstacle is usually easily overcome. Most people find that the group therapy experience is supportive and provides an atmosphere conducive for expression and change. Group therapy is usually less expensive than individual therapy—another inducement for the older adult with limited financial resources.

With all types of psychotherapy, it is vital that the therapist with whom the patient and family are working be someone who understands the issues involved in normal aging and is experienced in doing psychotherapy with older adults. We all become more complex as we age and the interplay of biological, social, medical, and psychological factors must be considered in all therapeutic ventures.

Medications

The development and use of specific medications over the past 30 years has revolutionized the treatment of depression. They are not panaceas, but when judiciously prescribed various medications can make the difference between a person being able to function and being grossly distressed. People often have psychosocial issues and/or upsetting longstanding patterns of relating or behaving that can be worked through in psychotherapy more easily when the more disturbing symptoms of depression are relieved with the help of medications. *People with major depressive or manic episodes usually require medication at some time in a successful treatment program.*

The medications most frequently used for affective disorders include:

tricyclic antidepressants and related medications,

lithium,

minor tranquilizers,

major tranquilizers,

monamine oxidase inhibitors,

stimulants, and

sleep-inducing drugs.

I will describe the uses and side effects of each group to familiarize you with the possible treatments that might be suggested for you or a family member. Before prescribing any medication for depression the physician will have performed or will have access to the history, physical examination, and laboratory data accumulated in the evaluation. This is crucial in making decisions about the choice of medications and in monitoring certain possible side effects. In addition, no physician would want to only be treating a depression when other medical problems existed.

Tricyclic Antidepressants

The "tricyclics" are the most commonly used antidepressant medications. This group of drugs is so named because the chemical structures of its compounds include three rings. There are up to twenty different medications in this or closely related categories. The tricyclics most commonly used for elderly patients include nortriptyline (Aventyl, Pamelor), desipramine (Norpramin, Pertofrane), imipramine (Torfranil and others), amitriptyline (Elavil and others), and doxepin (Sinequan and Adapin). Trazodone (Desyrel) is an antidepressant medication, commonly prescribed, but not related to the tricyclics. They all appear to work by affecting the brain chemicals, neurotransmitters, which regulate the transmission of nerve impulses in the brain. Evidence suggests that the amounts of these neurotransmitters are decreased in cases of depression. The antidepressant medications are generally similar in their effectiveness in reducing depression, but their side effects vary. Treating the elderly with medications requires a careful balance between maximizing effectiveness and minimizing side effects.

The presence of adverse side effects may determine whether a patient will agree to begin and then stay with treatment, and physicians should warn the patient and family about them and suggest some ways of dealing with them. Common undesirable side effects include drowsiness, dryness of the mouth, constipation, increased heart rate, difficulty urinating (more commonly in men), and light-headedness when standing up quickly from sitting or lying positions. Many of these effects will decrease after several days or a week of treatment, others can be minimized with some assistance, and some will require that another medication be substituted. Patients, family members, and clinicians should make great efforts to deal with the side effects, when present, and not give up hope. Since the beneficial effects of the medication may not be apparent for one to two weeks and the side effects are most prominent early in the therapy, many patients get discouraged and want to stop the therapy. In the long run, the beneficial effects of the antidepressants usually far outweigh the difficulties and it is normally worth tolerating the short-term side effects for the longer-term relief.

Some patients with certain underlying medical problems, such as heart and liver disorders, either will not be able to take tricyclic medications or will require special monitoring in the form of more frequent visits or blood tests.

Older adults generally need smaller doses of medications than do younger people because aging changes the absorption, metabolizing, and excretion of drugs. Most of these medications can be taken in a single dose in the evening, so that many of the side effects occur during sleep and are less problematic to the patient's daily functioning. In addition, the patient only has to remember to take the medicine once a day. This is a definite advantage to elderly patients, who are often taking several or many medications on complicated schedules. In rare cases, the antidepressants will stimulate some patients, causing them to feel too awake to sleep. In those situations the physician may choose to prescribe the medication for use in the morning or in a divided dose throughout the day. Although some general patterns are predictable in the use of medications, every patient's treatment has to be individualized to achieve the best results. Physicians with experience in the use of antidepressants for the elderly will feel comfortable enough to change dosages and types of drugs as necessary. In spite of the profound symptoms and the feelings of helplessness of the patient and family members, they must be patient with the physician's efforts to try various medications to obtain optimum relief. It is also vital for the physician to be patient, to increase the doses maximally, and to give the depressed person the several weeks that are often required to reach the proper drug levels to get the desired results.

After a patient begins taking a tricyclic antidepressant, it generally takes between one week and several weeks for a maximal therapeutic effect. After several days, however, the patient may feel calmer and sleep better. Gradually, the patient will experience greater interest in doing things, improved appetite, and a generally improved mood. Physicians primarily monitor the benefit of the medications by the clinical response of the patient. At times they may check the amount of drug in a patient by doing a blood test. At times they may want to do other blood tests to check kidney, liver, thyroid, and other functions as treatment proceeds. Patients who respond well to treatment say that they feel "like a new person," "like I've been brought back to life." Antidepressants are not "uppers" and should not result in a high. Symptoms of euphoria or elation are not desirable and should be reported to the prescribing physician.

Antidepressant medications must be taken continuously so that a high enough level of the medication in the blood is achieved. Unlike most medications, antidepressants usually take one to three weeks to produce a full therapeutic effect and several weeks for the therapeutic effect to wear off once the medication is stopped. This long wait for results often makes it difficult for the patient to see the cause and effect relationship that is so obvious with aspirin and antibiotics. Similarly, the principle of taking the medication only when upset, the way one takes aspirin for an ache, does not apply to antidepressants. Once a patient starts on antidepressant drugs, it is desirable to continue taking them as prescribed for at least six months. They are not addictive. No one likes to take medications and one of the most difficult problems that clinicians face in the treatment of depression with medication is the desire of the patient to stop the drug. We hear continually, "After all, I feel so good now. Why should I continue taking a drug?" Just as hypertensive patients must continue to take their medication, it is imperative that depressed patients continue with their medications. The decision to stop the medication must be made with the physician and the dose must be tapered carefully over several weeks. Neither the patient nor any family member should change dosage or type of medication without speaking with the prescribing physician. Antidepressants are highly effective and generally safe medications, but are also potentially dangerous when used carelessly.

Lithium

Lithium is one of the "miracle" drugs of the twentieth century. Introduced in the late 1960s and popularized since the early 1970s, lithium is an element similar to sodium and potassium. Lithium has been vital to the treatment of both bipolar disorders and recurrent depression. Lithium is highly effective in leveling off or normalizing the ups and downs of people with bipolar disorders. In 70 to 80 percent of people suffering with manic–depressive symptoms, lithium provides a permanent remission as long as the medication is continued. It is highly effective in leveling the moods of people who are referred to as "cyclothymic"—having cyclical mood swings that are not as extreme or intense as those of bipolar patients. Lithium is also used to treat patients with chronic or repetitive depressive episodes (without manic phases). Every patient with mood swings that interfere with everyday functioning on the job or in the family should be tried on a course of lithium unless cardiac, kidney, or other metabolic illnesses contraindicate its use, or unless the patient or a family member cannot be trusted to administer the medicine as prescribed. Lithium treatment can be combined with psychotherapy of various types, and in fact the effects of lithium often allow the patient to be more receptive to a talking therapy approach.

Many people, including some in the medical professions, think of lithium treatment as an extreme course. It is not. After some preliminary laboratory studies that are included in the blood tests previously mentioned, the patient is started on a small dose, given orally in pills, twice or three times per day. As with all other medications, dosages for the elderly are smaller and the physician should be aware of other drugs and medical illnesses that might be factors in the treatment. Lithium treatment necessitates periodic blood tests to monitor the level of lithium in the blood stream. At first this check needs to be done after a few days, then once a week for several weeks. After the dose is stabilized blood tests should be done once a month, and after several months less frequently. The blood tests can be done at any doctor's office, laboratory, or hospital and are not major impositions compared to the enormous benefit derived from this excellent treatment. Therapeutic blood levels range from 0.5 to 1.5 nanograms per milliliter of blood. In the elderly we aim for levels close to the low end of the range to minimize the side effects. The administration and monitoring of lithium should be done by a psychiatrist who is experienced in using the drug, particularly with the elderly. There is usually no problem locating such a person in most communities because lithium has become a valued part of treatment planning for most psychiatrists. Patients for whom lithium is effective will probably have to take it for the rest of their lives to prevent the recurrence of symptoms.

Many famous and successful people in the arts, show business, and industry have spoken out publicly about the benefits of lithium in treating their bipolar disorders. They point out that people who are manic often feel very good, maybe even the best they've ever felt. This issue presents a real challenge for psychiatrists and other clinicians who attempt to demonstrate to patients that they are out of control, impulsive, and so on, and therefore might benefit from treatment with lithium.

Side effects from lithium are minimal and if monitored properly there are almost no complications. It is generally a safer medication than the tricyclic antidepressants that are so commonly prescribed. Some patients complain of weight gain or muscle spasms. Lithium can also induce changes in thyroid functioning, and this must be routinely monitored. These changes are reversible. High levels of lithium in the blood can result in confusion, with slurred speech, loss of balance, and drowsiness. Family members should be alert to these possibilities. Patients who are taking diuretics for high blood pressure or heart disease need special attention when taking lithium and the prescribing physician will monitor those people more closely. Patients who take lithium should maintain a normal diet with adequate fluid intake.

Lithium was originally used for the treatment and prevention of the manic phase of bipolar disorders. In the past ten years it also has been demonstrated to be useful in preventing cyclical and chronic depressions, even when there is no history of manic episodes, and in treating people with cyclothymic disorders. Lithium is an effective adjunct to the tricyclics, and when used in combination with them seems to improve the benefits of tricyclics in the treatment of depression. Lithium can also be prescribed in combination with tranquilizers, particularly when severe agitation and psychotic symptoms such as hallucinations or delusions accompany mood swings. Lithium is not prescribed frequently enough, particularly with the elderly. When used with care, it is entirely safe and effective as a treatment and in the prevention of some of the most disabling and dangerous disorders that physicians treat.

Minor Tranquilizers

The minor tranquilizers are antianxiety drugs. They are generally prescribed for symptoms of agitation, tension, and subjective feelings of nervousness. The benzodiazepines are the most popular subgroup of minor tranquilizers and are represented by diazepam (Valium), oxazepam (Serax), lorazepam (Ativan), and others. These medications are widely prescribed by the medical profession and many have become household names. They are often used for anxiety, which may sometimes really be an agitated depression—a common condition in the elderly, in which the depressive symptoms are mixed with or overpowered by a highly anxious state. The minor tranquilizers are most useful for short-term anxiety states, crisis situations, and in detoxifying people from alcohol. They are potentially addictive and should be used with care if they are prescribed over long periods of time or in high doses. They are also potential depressants. In addition, the longer-acting members of the drug family, such as diazepam (Valium), tend to accumulate in the blood stream of older people and may be responsible for a chronic confused state in elderly patients, particularly those with pre-existing cognitive deficits. Some of the disorientation and confusion in hospitalized and medical and surgical patients is due to treatment for anxiety and to sedation with longer-acting benzodiazepines. Except for acute anxiety states, agitation accompanying depressions, and alcohol detoxification, this group of medications generally has little use in the treatment of depression in the elderly.

One possible exception to the last statement is a relatively new drug called alprazolam (Xanax). Although it is a member of the benzodiazepine antianxiety family, unlike other members of that group it has some antidepressant properties and is used by some physicians for the treatment of depression. It may have some advantages over other antidepressants in having fewer side effects, but many doctors are still concerned about dependence and problems with withdrawal from the medication.

These concerns can only be answered after several years of use in a large older adult population.

Major Tranquilizers

The major tranquilizers, or "antipsychotic" drugs, are highly effective in treating the severe agitation and/or psychotic symptoms—hallucinations and delusions—that often accompany a major depressive or manic episode in the elderly. An antidepressant and an antipsychotic are frequently combined in treating these situations. Although the combination increases the possibilities of side effects such as dryness of the mouth, constipation, blurred vision, and urinary symptoms, the therapeutic benefits are significant. The two types of medication often bring about a remission that would be impossible to achieve using either medicine alone. Because they sometimes cause drowsiness, the major tranquilizers are also useful as sedatives when sleep difficulties are a problem. They induce sleep and are not known to be addictive. The physician must be alert to the presence of side effects that are distressing to the patient and modify dosages or institute other measures as necessary. Two drugs in this group that are commonly used for the elderly are thioridazine (Mellaril) and haloperidol (Haldol).

Monoamine Oxidase (MAO) Inhibitors

The MAO inhibitors are another class of antidepressants that increase certain neurotransmitters in the brain. They inhibit an enzyme that metabolizes those brain chemicals. The MAO inhibitors are generally regarded as secondary choices as antidepressants, especially in the elderly. These medications have many of the same side effects as the tricyclics and also necessitate certain dietary and medication restrictions. MAOs are used far more commonly in younger people, for whom they have been demonstrated to be effective. There is less clinical and research experience with MAOs in older adults. They should be tried, however, if the tricyclics fail to produce relief.

Stimulants

Although not true antidepressants, the stimulant drugs, of which methylphenidate (Ritalin) is the most popular, have a role in activating very lethargic, apathetic patients who are just beginning tricyclic therapy. Stimulants are also useful in patients who have been unresponsive to antidepressants or cannot tolerate more traditional antidepressant medications because of medical complications or underlying problems that preclude the use of tricyclics or MAOs. Stimulants are generally given in small doses early in the day, so as not to interfere with sleep. They have few side effects and are often effective within several days. Stimulants are particularly useful when depression is due to a medical crisis and when there is some indication that the depression might resolve quickly. They are not recommended for long-term use. Stimulants have several drawbacks including a brief duration of action, potential side effects of insomnia, appetite loss and hyperactivity, and a tendency to cause a rebound to depression in some cases.

Sleep-Inducing Drugs

Except for very short-term (one week) use, I do not generally recommend the prescription of sedative-hypnotic medications (sleeping pills). Although everyone is distressed when insomnia is a problem, it is crucial to first examine the possible causes of sleeplessness and to try possible nonmedication remedies. If depression or a bipolar disorder is present, antidepressants and/or major tranquilizers and psychotherapy may be indicated and will usually treat the sleep problem as well as the mood disorder. Sleeping pills are dangerous because they are habit-forming, lethal in overdoses, and are depressants. Barbiturates, the favorite sedative-hypnotics of the last generation of physicians and patients, are specifically contraindicated for all of these reasons. If a short-term sleep-inducing medication is required, a short-acting benzodiazepine, such as triazolam (Halcion), may be tried. These medications work quickly to induce sleep and are mostly cleared from the patient's blood stream after 6 to 8 hours so that no hang-over results. Another relatively safe drug of many years' use is chloral hydrate. Again, these medications should be used with caution and for brief periods. An individual patient may have an idiosyncratic reaction to any of the drugs in this group and may be stimulated rather than sedated.

Combinations of Medications

As clinicians have come to use medications more widely for the treatment of depression and now see the many ways in which the person's biology effects and is affected by depression, they have derived some innovative treatment techniques.

Various of the medications mentioned previously can be used judiciously in combination when one alone, combined with psychotherapy, does not alleviate the depressive symptoms. Tricyclic antidepressants, lithium, monoamine oxidase inhibitors, and major tranquilizers have all been used in various combinations. In addition, thyroid hormone and some anticonvulsants (i.e., Tegretol) have been tried in very resistant situations.

Although the treatment of depression with medications is still evolving as we learn more about the subtle interactions of biological and environmental factors, medications are now essential in the treatment of older adults with depression and should be judiciously prescribed.

Electroconvulsive Therapy (ECT)

The idea of ECT ("shock") therapy is frightening to most laymen, evoking fears of primitive torture. In fact, ECT is one of the most effective treatments for severe depression and may be life-saving in certain situations. It is almost always administered in a hospital setting, particularly with the elderly, and the technique used makes it safe, humane, effective, and minimizes side effects.

Although in most situations patients are first treated with antidepressant medications and psychotherapy, ECT is often more effective in the severely depressed older adult than either of the above. ECT works quickly, often within a week, while medications may take several weeks to be beneficial. ECT is particularly useful when the patient is extremely regressed and withdrawn, is not eating, is dangerously suicidal, or is tortured by the psychotic symptoms of delusions and hallucinations. It may also be safer than medications when a patient is medically ill and antidepressants are contraindicated.

ECT is usually used for an acute depressive episode. Unlike antidepressant medications, there is no evidence that ECT prevents future depressions. Thus, patients often need maintenance on antidepressant medications and/or lithium after an episode in order to help prevent future symptoms. ECT can be used effectively with repeated depressions and many patients come to prefer it to other treatment options.

ECT is administered after the patient is given a short-acting anesthetic and a muscle relaxant drug. An electrode or a small metal disc is applied to one or both temples and an electrical current is briefly given from a special machine. Because the patient has taken a muscle relaxant, there is little discernible convulsion, except for some muscle contraction in the hands and feet, which lasts less than a minute. The patient is allowed to wake up and usually experiences some confusion and/or memory loss for a few hours. Treatments are given two to four times per week for a total of five to twelve treatments.

Some patients may suffer some impaired memory for some weeks or months, but this is usually significant and long-lasting only in people who were previously demented. There is a small incidence of heart rhythm disturbances, headaches, and rare fractures of the spinal column especially where there is pre-existing osteosporosis. These risks have to be weighed against the sometimes life-saving benefits that result from ECT when it is used in patients with severely disabling depression.

When patients are well selected—usually after other treatments are attempted—ECT can yield dramatic results in treating a major depressive episode. I am reminded of an elderly gentleman on a medical ward of a university hospital who had stopped eating and speaking, was maintained on intravenous fluids, and behaved as if he was preparing to die. He had a history of previous depressions and rather severe heart disease, which precluded the use of antidepressant medications. Stimulant drugs in small doses produced no effect, and he was resistant to any kind of psychotherapy. After his cardiac problems were stabilized he steadfastly refused further treatment, and revealed that he had thought he would die during his hospitalization and wanted that to happen. He thought that his life was over and had visions that "the Lord is coming to take me." Efforts to convince him to try ECT were in vain until he developed a rather sudden and intense fascination with an older woman who cleaned the hospital unit and who reminded him of his deceased wife. At times it seemed to him that this woman was his wife. He seemed to have a new reason to live and agreed to have ECT. After two treatments his mood lifted considerably, his vigor increased, and he became verbal and coherent. He suffered minimal memory impairment, but was able, after two additional treatments, to return to his apartment in a retirement center and to function more independently than he had in a year. We never learned what happened to his relationship with his new friend!

Hospitalization

To hospitalize or not? Most older adults with depression can be treated as out-patients; they do not require hospitalization. When someone does need to be hospitalized for depression, the need is often clear to the patient, and it is almost always apparent to the family that a change of therapeutic environment is necessary. Frequently the family is exhausted or extremely worried about a loved one who is depressed and they approach the therapist to pursue hospitalization. That point of exhaustion or worry is important for the therapist to know about. For the therapist, these signs are a concrete indication of what the family has been up against, what their resources are, and how the patient's status has changed. It is crucial that family members and friends aggressively pursue the clinicians involved in the care of their loved ones, especially when conditions have changed for the worse.

What are the options for hospitalization? The possibilities for in-patient treatment for depression include the psychiatric units of general or university hospitals, private psychiatric hospitals, and public hospitals. As with all medical problems, the patient should be treated at the closest facility that is best able to treat the problem and is at the same time financially feasible. In some cities, hospitals now have special geriatric units or doctors who are specially trained in geriatrics and geriatric psychiatry. Sometimes these specialists can serve as consultants to the other available hospitals.

Why hospitalize? There are several major reasons to seek inpatient treatment, including:

1. To perform extended diagnostic evaluations. Particularly in the elderly, medical issues may complicate the diagnosis and treatment of depression. The hospital setting may be required to carefully observe the patient and to perform certain assessment procedures that are more easily accomplished on a psychiatric unit.

2. To use treatments in a highly supervised setting. In the frail older adult, where there are medical complications or where several treatment attempts have failed, hospitalization is indicated. Sometimes combinations of medications

for medical and psychiatric conditions need to be administered in a controlled atmosphere.

3. To protect a person from suicide, homicide, severe agitation, or behaviors that result from psychotic thinking. The secure nature of a psychiatric unit or hospital can help prevent some of the catastrophic possibilities mentioned above. No family setting is physically or psychologically equipped to deal effectively with these problems.

4. To provide the family or other care-givers with some relief or respite from their care of the patient. Family members can easily be exhausted by a demanding, agitated, and/or severely depressed person in their midst and may need relief. Hospitalization may be the only realistic option with certain patients and in certain families.

The hospital setting provides the clinician with a valuable tool in the diagnosis and treatment of depression in the elderly. No clinician takes this step lightly because of the emotional and financial considerations involved in hospitalization. Although often frightened by the prospect, the patient and family usually feel quite relieved that they are receiving more intensive care than can be provided in an out-patient setting.

The treatment of depression in the older adult is complex, involving a number of possible therapies that may be used alone or in combination. The clinician must be versatile, flexible, and knowledgeable. He or she must know when to recommend a consultation with a colleague who may have specialized knowledge or skill with a particular therapy or area of expertise. The family can also request that kind of additional intervention.

The most important point to be drawn from this chapter is that depression is a potentially treatable disorder in the vast majority of affected people. Proper treatment must be sought, attempted, and vigorously pursued without the prejudice that the elderly person is entitled to be depressed. This notion would never be tolerated in a young man or woman.

After treatment is instituted and the patient is stabilized, the patient and the family must be diligent in following the recommendations of the therapist in the months and years ahead. It is tempting to stop treatment because one is feeling so well. Depression is often a chronic and recurrent disorder. Treatment is prescribed to deal with a particular episode and also to minimize future episodes that may be disabling. To accomplish these goals treatment that has been started successfully *must* be continued, and should be modified and adjusted only under the expert supervision of a clinician who has been actively involved with the patient.

8

The Family

Mr. H was a pleasant 81-year-old man who had functioned in what appeared to his family to be a "normal" manner until his wife's death, two years before he sought treatment. After her sudden death, Mr. H became unable to cope with day-to-day responsibilities and activities. He didn't clean his apartment and "forgot" whether or not he had food in the refrigerator. He didn't want to be left alone in his apartment, so he made efforts to have people take him places. He stopped driving his car, although his vision, hearing, and response time were adequate. He said that he worried too much to drive. He wasn't sleeping well, had lost fifteen pounds in the past year, and was plagued by worries of financial disaster. He complained to his son and daughter-in-law about his indigestion and headaches, but his physician could not find a treatable medical illness. Mr. H felt that his family didn't visit enough. Recently, he had thought that maybe he would be "better off dead." After all, he wasn't "worth anything to anyone."

Mr. H's immediate family consisted of his son, daughter-in-law, and their two children who lived in the same city, and a daughter, son-in-law, and their three children who lived 2,000 miles away. Mr. H also had an older sister living in a nursing home nearby, but he had rarely visited her in the past year.

Mr. H's grandchildren had previously enjoyed spending weekends at his apartment. "It was a special treat." He let them stay up late on Saturday night and even cooked special foods for them. "Lately he hasn't been that much fun." He seemed to be preoccupied, worried, and sad. He didn't seem interested in their studies, achievements, or problems. "He isn't himself!" The grandchildren saw Mr. H less frequently; they didn't want to spend a whole day with him and he didn't "feel up to having them." They all felt as if something had been lost.

Mr. H's deterioration had a significant effect on his family and the members of his family had affected him. His children, living near and far, were frustrated, angry, sad, guilty, and fearful. They didn't know how to help him and whatever they attempted to do or say didn't seem to have more than a temporary effect on his disposition. They were angry that their children were deprived of an active, loving, happy grandfather. They were also angry that they had to spend so much time worrying about their father, and they were sad that he was so tortured and helpless when "there's so much to enjoy." They felt guilty that they had feelings other than ones of great devotion, especially since Mr. H had told them many stories of his devotion to his sick mother. They cared very much for him, wanted him to be part of their lives, but not to consume their lives. They feared the unknowns of his disorder: Would he ever get better? Would he be a chronic invalid? What were the effects of treatment? Would their lives be run by his depression?

T HE issues raised by this vignette are typical of what a psychiatrist hears from a family that has been trying to cope with depression in an older adult relative. All families are stressed when they attempt to deal with concerns like those Mr. H presented to his family. The depressed older person is regressed (i.e., child-like, dependent, demanding) and needy, and the family experiences the sadness, anger, guilt, and fears that are common when one has to deal with any chronic or catastrophic illness in a family member. A vicious cycle can be set up, in which the prospective patient alienates the very people who can be of the most assistance to him or her. Mr. H desperately wanted more from his family, but his symptoms of withdrawal, sadness, worrying, and complaining made him difficult for them to be with, and they began to shun an unpleasant situation by avoiding him. Although a depressed person usually does not take on a new personality, the stress of the disorder and the inherent regression can, in addition to the actual symptoms of depression, bring out some of the person's worst characteristics. It is helpful, but not always possible, if one or more of the family members can—in spite of their intense and varied emotions—stay aware of the fact that dad or mom or grandma has a disorder, an illness that is producing his or her symptoms and requires professional attention.

The Family's Role in Treatment

What, then, can the family do in this situation? As mentioned throughout this book, a vital role that the family plays is *observation*. Particularly when a depressed person is able to cover up to the external world, close family members may be the only people who really know what he or she is like. It is tempting for everyone to deny dreadful symptoms in a loved one, especially when there has been a dramatic change in behavior or functioning. The next step the family can take is the *initiation of treatment*. Older adults usually get to medical or mental health professionals for psychological problems because someone pushes them to do so. Without a frustrated but caring son and daughter, Mr. H might not have gotten an evaluation, accurate diagnosis, and proper treatment. Sometimes this requires the kind of forceful *confrontation* that was previously discussed.

As the work-up proceeded, Mr. H's son wondered whether he should have invited his father to move into his house after his mother's death. Would that have prevented the deterioration? Should he and his family have spent more time with him? Is there anything he or his sister could have done? They did care about him, but he had become "difficult." There are no certain answers to these questions. We know that depression is caused by a combination of biological and environmental factors, but we don't know how much of each is necessary.

What is most important is that we recognize the signs and symptoms of depression in people who are close to us, so that we can get them the best possible care—without self-reproach about what should have been done.

After helping to initiate treatment, the family has a role in *supporting* and facilitating it. Clinicians often depend on the family to help an older patient get to appointments, take the medicine as prescribed, and make environmental changes. The family may also be involved in hiring supporting personnel, if necessary. Sometimes the family will decide that the older patient should or could move into the family house. That decision may be more easily accomplished if the patient's therapist or someone he or she recommends is available to help to deal with the transition. Another kind of transition may be the elderly patient's move to a senior citizens' residence or to a nursing home. The decisions concerning living arrangements obviously depend on such factors as the physical and mental health of the patient, financial considerations, social and environmental issues, and the state of the supporting family and friends. These decisions affect the whole family and should be talked through with the physician or mental health professional who is involved with the patient.

Support for a depressed parent or friend does not mean martyrdom. Although one may extend oneself in behalf of another, it is crucial that the helping person know his or her limits. Everyone's tolerance for such things is different. But, a person who is so giving and so available that he or she feels abused will have great difficulty in continuing a supportive relationship on any basis, and the depressed person will then experience that withdrawal as another loss.

In addition to some of the practical ways in which the family supports treatment, family members may often be adjuncts to the ongoing therapy. One or more family members may be seen periodically with the identified patient, or they may be seen alone to inform the therapist of things that might not otherwise be revealed or to deal with problems that would not be discussed without their involvement. Sometimes the therapist will recommend that one or more of the family members also seek therapy to work out issues that might have been provoked by the crisis that depression in a family can bring. Another possibility is that "family therapy" will be recommended, in which all or part of the family can be seen together with a therapist to work out family stresses, to support family strengths, or to better understand the ways in which the family functions.

Family therapy can be approached using several different techniques. Some therapists focus more on communication, while others concentrate on family history and dynamics. Regardless of a particular therapist's technique, certain major themes should be addressed to help the family, including the depressed person, function better.

One of the immediate issues that arises in families with dysfunctional members is the need for support for the family. Bringing an outsider, a therapist, into the family system gives the new person the opportunity to add support that the family may desperately need by the time therapy is sought. Incidentally, the therapist must be careful to remain somewhat of an "outsider" to the family; he or she must not become embroiled in the family's turmoil, but must observe it and attempt to help clarify it. The therapist assists by allowing family members to talk to each other—to say and to hear things more clearly. The therapist can offer concrete information about depression and its treatment. It is important for the family members to understand the problem as a disorder that has causes, signs and symptoms, and treatment possibilities. Family members might be anxious about the familial and genetic aspects of depression and the therapist should be able to respond to such concerns, whether explicit or implicit.

The therapist can give permission to family members to express previously "unexpressable" feelings and thoughts. The family members may feel guilty about their anger, disgust, and frustration with the situation and need to see that those are normal and understandable emotions. They also need to be able to talk about their sadness, love, and concern. Both of these sets of feelings are difficult for some people to discuss without an outside person who allows them to be talked out.

Children, no matter what their ages, are used to the idea that their parents take care of them. A medical or psychological disorder in an older adult family member may produce a temporary or more long-standing role reversal in which the adult child must assume a primary caretaking role. This may cause significant anxiety in all concerned. Acknowledging and understanding the anxiety-provoking role reversal may result in an easier relationship between parent and child.

Sometimes families inadvertently encourage the depression and its accompanying dysfunction in one person in order to hide even more distressing problems within the family. In these families, the therapist's job entails ferreting out the family dynamics so that one person doesn't get blamed for all the family troubles and become the family scapegoat.

The family therapist assesses family strengths and weaknesses, and uses that knowledge to help the family deal with the stresses of depression in terms of the members' own assets and limitations. Every family has rituals and values that affect its general functioning and, more specifically, has ways of dealing with the elderly and the ill members within the family. The family functions within its longstanding healthy or unhealthy patterns of behavior, communication, and roles. Sometimes family patterns can be somewhat modified in the face of stress and the therapist can help the family see where those patterns are working well and where they need change. The therapist can assist with such changes.

> Mr. H was seen weekly together with several members of his extended family over three months, in addition to his own individual psychotherapy sessions. Within the context of the family sessions Mr. H was able to more clearly and directly express his sense of loss and his need for greater involvement

with his children. He had always had difficulty in asking for things—he had been the independent one, the doer in the family—but now he needed them and finally could ask. His children and grandchildren responded with relief that he could be so direct, but they also set limits on how much of his invalidism they would tolerate. In essence a bargain was struck between Mr. H and his family, and much of the prior frustration and anger was dissipated. Mr. H's individual therapy and medication facilitated his increased ability to function and he gradually resumed his interests and activities.

The family can become more responsible for the problems within it, especially if the members feel the support and understanding of an available professional. Whether the issues involve setting limits on a depressed patient's intolerable behavior, responding to a grandparent's need for more time and attention, watching for potential suicidal behavior in a loved one, or making the plans for hospitalization or nursing home placement, the family can mobilize to function in ways that might not have been possible without the intervention of a therapist.

The Person Without a Family

Most elderly adults have some family or close friends on whom they can depend in times of need. But some people grow old in relative isolation and therefore may have more difficulty when they are physically or emotionally ill. After such an elderly person has been hospitalized for surgery or a medical illness, physicians may have to make special arrangements with visiting nurse services or with convalescent care centers to facilitate the recuperation of someone who doesn't have available family or friends.

When more isolated elderly people have psychological problems, they may not come to medical attention unless they seek it on their own initiative. Although I have emphasized the role of family members in helping to obtain psychological care for their relatives, many people—with and without families—do seek assistance on their own. Others may get help through the intervention of local agency representatives, neighbors, interested storekeepers, community leaders, clergymen, or others with whom they have contact. One 88-year-old former music teacher with no family was brought to a geriatric clinic by two former students who visited her frequently. Although they were unable to provide a place for her in their own homes, they helped her find a senior citizens' residence that would provide more support services for her than her rather impersonal apartment house. In the course of a brief psychotherapy the older woman reminisced about her work over 50 years with many hundreds of students, some of whom she had clearly adopted as her "family." Until this time of need she saw herself as a relatively isolated person who had lost everything because she could no longer teach music to young people. In fact, the experience of having her students' support reinforced a sense of self-esteem that she had lost or forgotten over her years of retirement, and provided her with some practical assistance in getting resettled.

Afterword:
Looking Forward

A T the age of 65 the average person has a life expectancy of another 15 or 20 years. At age 75 that person has 10 or 15 years. Those can be enjoyable, productive, and fulfilling years. Depression can make them a series of nightmares.

Depression is a disorder and not an acceptable way of life or an inevitable state for older adults. It is the most common disorder for which elderly people seek help, although their complaints may be hidden behind the cloak of physical symptoms, denial, and fear that "this is what it is to be old." Although most older people are healthy, physically and psychologically, depression in one form or another may affect up to 20 percent of the people over 65 years of age; many are severely affected.

Elderly people are more complex biologically, socially, and psychologically than any other age group; furthermore, a network of factors conspire to predispose many older adults to depression. These include biological changes in the body, including the brain; multiple losses; social isolation; medical conditions and their treatments; and a sense of impending crisis or death. Vulnerability to depression is determined by the balance between personal strengths and good fortune on the one hand, and life crises and biological predispositions on the other.

The diagnosis of depression in the elderly requires careful assessment of a large number of factors. Many depressed older adults are undiagnosed, misdiagnosed, and—most unfortunately—untreated. Depression has to be distinguished from the dementias, which are also common in the elderly, and from other medical conditions.

Depression at any age is a treatable disorder—one of the most treatable problems that physicians and other clinicians see. Depression in the elderly is no exception. Mild depression may be helped by a variety of home remedies, including activities, socialization, exercise, and the supportive concern of family and friends. More severe depression requires a combination of psychotherapy and medication administered by psychiatrists or other therapists who understand the special issues confronted by the elderly and the interplay between medical and psychological issues.

Depression is a chronic disorder, in some ways like heart disease and diabetes, but in other ways quite different. Like those, depression can have a variable course. It may require ongoing maintenance treatment, but unlike some chronic medical problems, in many people an episode of depression may never be followed by another or there can be gaps of many years. Depression, if treated, is not life-threatening. Once depression is stabilized, an older person can look forward to an otherwise normal life. "Getting old" cannot be treated, the disorder of depression can. It is worth making the effort.

Related Readings

Enjoy Old Age, B.F. Skinner and M.E. Vaughan. Warner Books, New York, 1983.

A practical guide to living more fully in the later years.

Moodswing, Ronald R. Fieve. Bantam Books, New York, 1975.

A description of the chemical treatment of moodswings, particularly the use of lithium.

The 36-Hour Day, Nancy L. Mace and Peter V. Rabins. Johns Hopkins University Press, Baltimore, 1981.

A family guide for caring for people with Alzheimer's disease and related illnesses.

Index

About the Author

NATHAN BILLIG, M.D., was born in New York City and was educated at Queens College of the City University of New York and the State University of New York Upstate Medical Center. His postgraduate medical education in psychiatry was obtained at the Bronx Municipal Hospital Center/ Albert Einstein College of Medicine and the Georgetown University Medical Center.

Dr. Billig has practiced and taught psychiatry in Washington, D.C., for over 15 years. He is an associate professor of psychiatry and director of the Geriatric Psychiatry Program at the Georgetown University Medical Center, Washington, D.C. In addition to his work with the elderly, Dr. Billig is involved in psychotherapy with young adults and the psychological aspects of physical disease.